Visions
for a Compassionate
America

Luigi Morelli

OPEN BOOK EDITIONS
A Berrett-Koehler Partner | iUniverse®

VISIONS FOR A COMPASSIONATE AMERICA

iUniverse books may be ordered through booksellers or by contacting:

iUniverse
1663 Liberty Drive
Bloomington, IN 47403
www.iuniverse.com
1-800-Authors (1-800-288-4677)

ISBN: 978-1-4917-6637-8 (sc)
ISBN: 978-1-4917-6638-5 (e)

Print information available on the last page.

iUniverse rev. date: 6/2/2015

Contents

Introduction

The American Dream gave birth to the ideals of freedom from government oppression, equal rights bestowed on individuals by the Declaration of Independence, and the opportunity to rise above one's origins. This is what I explored in *Legends and Stories for a Compassionate America*, in vignettes that are like fragments of the American kaleidoscope. But what of the dream at present?

America is a land of extremes. And there are extreme forces that are gathering strength and attempting to impose a retrograde movement toward a new capitalism of the Wild West. Strategies that have not worked in the past are being used more and more, being heaped up as the solution for the future: more fossil fuels, and more noxious ones at that, including more fracking and more pipelines to obtain our northern neighbors' tar sands oil; more environmental deregulation and environmental catastrophes; more business influence on government; more Wall Street deregulation and more income inequality; more central government and more global surveillance. The list could go on, and what it represents could be defined as a new category of national denial.

In the midst of these trends, talk of a level economic field, or of reviving the American middle class, becomes just that: empty talk. The numbers show that there is nothing, no matter how blatantly obvious, that cannot be ignored by those who wish to engage in denial. Climate change disruptions have made headlines for the last five to ten years if not longer. And quite consistent with the official denial, global climate change did not figure in the debates of the two American presidential candidates in 2012.

Yet denial is not a matter of culture, parties, or segments of the population alone. It is the unavoidable companion of fear and loss of meaning and hope. It is the drama on the stage of the soul, which presents itself to America and to the world at large. We all struggle as individuals to find meaning and to rescue hope; hence, we all know the danger of denial. We cannot forge a new future without facing and accepting the powerlessness of the present.

Fear and denial are the weapons of choice of those interests who want to cling to the past or offer an empty future in which the human being has no place. Denial obscures the seeds of hope that spring all around us, makes them look like mere aberrations, belittles them constantly; it dulls our perceptions, distracts our gaze, dims our interest or enthusiasm, offers us degrading distractions instead; it erases the field of possibility that is always present in living reality. It finally renders us unable to see what is in front of our eyes.

Seeing more fully is the first goal of this book. If America is a land of contrast, what is the counter to all that has been exposed in the preceding paragraphs? People all over the world still naively look up to America for possibility, for something that is yet to come, and that defines the human experience more fully than it has yet been expressed. If America then is the land of contrasts, is it possible that something equally real and imbued with hope and promise also lives under the nightmarish reality that we face daily? I have spent decades recognizing the other forces that do not bind us either to the past or to a dehumanizing future. I live in the realization that there are many new ideas and visions that have power and substance that promise to rebuild reality all around us and make room for a fuller human being. This is the central object of this writing: to make room for the hundreds of visionaries who have struggled and still struggle to offer another idea of America to the world. Their presence is real; their gifts are tangible; their vision is wholesome. It is in the role of a witness that I bring the pieces of this vision to coalesce in these pages. My role is to show that there is a whole that is even larger than the parts, and that is the vision for a compassionate America.

I have shown how the American continent has been a land of extremes not just in the present but also in the millennia preceding our times. Legends of Maya, Incas, Aztecs, Iroquois, Hopi, and others talk about the worlds and epochs that have preceded our own and of their conclusions in times of great decadence. It was in the Americas that practices of live human sacrifice displayed unspeakable cruelty both more than two millennia ago and at the time of the Aztecs. These were times of great anguish. The chronicle of these times lies embedded in the puzzling language of myths and legends that need be decoded, in order to render to Americans, north and south, ownership of their history. Native American consciousness of the past lived in primeval images, whose ultimate meaning is lost to modern consciousness, and hence, there is a real disconnect between present American culture and its roots in Native America. I sought to read and understand American prehistory and early history in relation to North America and to South America in previous works. It is not necessary for the reading of this volume. However, if one took the time to enter the consciousness of legends and myths, the continuity of American history would become engrossing.

The dream and the nightmare have accompanied much of early American history already. Yet, also in America, the Maya, Inca, and Iroquois civilizations showed a way out of the despair, toward the light of new societies. They were the fruit of cultural revolutions and emerged as if out of nothing. Renewal arrived in the middle of the night, when hope seemed lost, through incredible individuals and events that defy our modern rationalistic mind-set.

But back to the present. It is easy to look back to the pages of our history and either idolize in empty praise or render relative all real accomplishments. The way out of this lies once again in seeing better, in looking at the facts and letting the facts reveal a picture, an image of what lies beyond the facts. And for certain, the elusive dream lies beyond quantifiable facts. This book continues where *Legends and Stories for a Compassionate America* left off. That first attempt sought to show the wholeness of the American Dream and its continuity. This book searches for the American Dream in its new, evolving version.

Chapter 1 offers a sobering look at present trends of a world run amok; it stares denial in the face. If we want to find a better future, let us face the depth of reality. Chapter 2 introduces the idea of cultural renewal as the real engine for more permanent social change. It looks at the work of those who have struggled to renew American culture, to offer a fuller picture and notion of what it means to go through the human adventure. They have tried to give us anew what religion or tradition offered us in the past. This is only a promising beginning. Parallel to that is the role of civil society as the vehicle for culture and the agent for lasting change.

So where do we place politics in the whole? Chapter 3 looks at what is the genius of America, its greatest gift to the world. It is the laboratory of ideas about how human beings can relate more fully to each other, be it in day-to-day dialogue or in the most elaborate decision-making challenges. It looks in great part at the possible revolution of a post-two-party system. Imagine a society that would work for all, and try to set aside clichés or skepticism. American "social technology," or tools for dialogue and deliberation, offers ideas and practices for tackling change at the level of communities, companies, and networks—ideas that have been tested over decades, even though the predominant narrative has placed them at the margins. And ideas have been tested or elaborated to bring this reality to the local, regional, and national levels.

And what about our economy? Can something bring change there? Chapter 4 explores how the ideas brought about in chapter 2 are impacting ways of doing business. Here vision extends to embracing sustainability and engaging business in collaboration with those sectors of society with which business continuously interacts. The chapter talks about all possible levels of private, nonprofit, and public-sector collaborations. This isn't just about business turned more human; rather, it is a whole other paradigm for a new economy. It spells the economy's subordination to society's goals in opposition to its present emancipation from other parts of society and its lack of moral responsibility.

And how do all parts fit into a whole? This is explored in chapter 5 through the work of American pioneers, past and present. Is there a more holistic way of looking at social change, one that is compatible with a future of increasing social and environmental challenges? How can we listen to what the future is asking of American and global citizens? How can we move away from the present day's increasingly sterile and dangerous polarization to a society that works for all? There must be an adventure of the mind before we turn to a concrete adventure. In conclusion, we will review the road map of the possible, the vision of a more compassionate America.

Chapter 1

A Distant Dream

The greatness of America lies not in being more enlightened than any other nation, but rather in her ability to repair her faults.
—Alexis de Tocqueville

*T*he present book is based on the premise that new, vigorous thinking is needed to address societal issues that are no longer approachable with thinking from the past. This is due in part to the complexity of issues we are facing as a nation and to the global dimension of crisis after crisis.

The United States is interlinked with global reality, both upstream and downstream. The American model of development gone global is in great part responsible for the global crisis. And climate change is one of these global consequences that has repercussions worldwide and is revisiting our country. Let us look at the world before we return home.

Climate Change and America

The World Wildlife Fund (WWF) publishes the *Living Planet Report*—now in its tenth edition—to record changes in wildlife populations. The 2014 Living Planet Index (LPI) measures the health of over 10,000 populations of more than 3,000 species. Between 1970 and 2010, the LPI shows a 52 percent decline; in other words, animal populations have been reduced to half what they were forty years ago.[1]

When we look at the rate of exploitation of the planet's resources, the WWF assesses that by 2008, human beings were using the equivalent of 1.5 planets to support their activities, not just consuming the accumulated interest of biological activity but actively destroying the capital, a trend that moves us away from any notion of sustainability.

Such is the disruption to the climate resulting from these suicidal practices that some 2.7 billion people live in areas where severe water shortages occur at least one month a year.[2]

According to a January 2005 study involving 95,000 participants from ninety-five countries, by 2010 temperatures were likely to rise by as much as 20 degrees Farhenheit.[3] From 1985 to 2005, temperatures in the Arctic rose eight times faster than during the previous one hundred years. Bringing all these findings closer to home, consider that in Alaska and western Canada, temperatures rose up to seven degrees Fahrenheit in the last sixty years.[4] At the latitude of the US Rockies, the lowest elevation for freezing moved upward by 500 feet from 1970 to 2005. There were 150 glaciers in Glacier National Park, where there are now less than thirty. And in the last century, New England precipitation has increased by 25 percent, while snowfall decreased by 15 percent from 1953 to 2005.[5]

Global climate is in part the result of economic globalization. And globalization is responsible for another trend: the exponential growth of economic disparity.

The Growing Economic Divide and the Justice Gap

The growing economic gap between developing countries and the Western world is mirrored in a staggering way in the income inequality of the United States. A few numbers speak to this reality very clearly. In 1995 the six-largest bank-holding companies in the United States held 17.1 percent of US GDP. When the 2008 financial crisis hit, this percentage had reached 55 percent; two years later, the combined assets of the holding companies were estimated at 64 percent of GDP.[6]

In the period from 2009 to 2012 alone, incomes of the top 1 percent of US earners grew by 31.4 percent, whereas incomes of the bottom 99 percent grew by only 0.4 percent. The top 1 percent captured 95 percent of the income gains in the first three years of the recovery. This is the very same top 1 percent who benefited from the 2008 financial bailouts and who now further consolidate their monopolistic power.[7]

Extending our gaze globally is just as revealing. In 2010 foreign exchange transactions worldwide reached the staggering amount of

US$1.5 quadrillion (4,500 trillion) against a meager US$20 trillion in international trade. Everything above this 0.4 percent amounts to purely speculative transactions, a reality of which we seldom speak.[8]

We can easily deduce from this information that in a system in which immense privilege is the norm, justice cannot remain unaffected. Let us remain within the world of banking to take a closer look at the growing "justice gap." Crimes that individuals commit and get punished for differ from the crimes of corporate America, which can buy itself economies of scale.

When the toxic mortgage securities started turning bad, investors lost faith in the banking system, and the housing crisis turned into the 2008 financial crisis that led to millions of home foreclosures. This did not lead to the expected consequences in the rule of law. In March 2013, Attorney General Eric Holder declared, "I am concerned that the size of some of these institutions becomes so large that it does become difficult for us to prosecute them when we are hit with indications that if you do prosecute, if you do bring a criminal charge, it will have a negative impact on the national economy, perhaps even the world economy."[9] Eric Holder was the same attorney general who had previously stated, "Not only the conduct of JPMorgan, it was the conduct of other banks doing similar kinds of things that led directly to the collapse of our economy in 2008 and in 2009."[10]

At the end of the year 2013, America witnessed one of its largest legal settlements in history: in agreeing to pay $13 billion to settle claims in the sale of mortgage securities to investors, JP Morgan Chase was admitting its guilt. Consider, though, that $7 billion of the settlement was tax-deductible, that no JP Morgan Chase executive was brought to justice, and that a securities fraud became a simple "overstating the quality of mortgages." The facts were withheld from public scrutiny and would have remained so were it not for the recent courageous exposure by Alayne Fleischmann, a lawyer formerly employed by JP Morgan Chase turned whistleblower.

The 2013 settlement was publicly hailed as a major victory in the fight to rein in banking abuse. Measure this more soberly against some important subsequent events. Within the month in which the settlement was announced, the stock of JPMorgan Chase rose by 6 percent, netting some $12 billion, or more than what the settlement had effectively cost. Within the same time span, Jamie Dimon, JP Morgan's CEO, was awarded a 74 percent raise by JP Morgan Chase's board, bringing his total compensation to $20 million. According to the *New York Times*, Jamie Dimon was rewarded by the board because he earned it "by acting as chief negotiator as JPMorgan worked out a string of banner government settlements."[11]

When privilege and impunity are the order of the day, no sector of society is spared. We will look next at health care and then at education, arguably two of the most important sectors to gauge the vibrancy of a society.

Health Care Out of Control

The growing economic divide forms the backdrop of many social problems. Health care is only one of them, but one of the best documented. Health care expenditures absorb some $1.8 trillion a year in the United States, which corresponds to 17.6 percent of the GDP in 2009.[12]

Let us place this in a global context. In 2008 health care in Canada absorbed some 9.9 percent of the country's GDP, and in the United Kingdom it absorbed 8.0 percent, in Germany 11.1 percent, and in Switzerland 11.5 percent. The figures translate to $5,700 per person in the United States versus $2,669 in Canada and $2,981 in the United Kingdom. And reform in this sector can be very expensive to push through the halls of Congress, especially if it has to curry favor with the senators sitting on the Senate Finance Committee, which is in charge of introducing new legislation on the matter. The Sunlight Foundation and OpenSecrets.org estimate that the health care and insurance industries have paid out contributions ranging from $650,000 to $9.5 million, with an average of 2.15 million paid to each of the twenty-three committee members.[13]

We may think that great progress has been made in the last few years, and that is partly true. The Affordable Care Act (ACA) was signed into law by President Obama in March 2010. It aimed at increasing the affordability of health insurance, expanding public and private insurance coverage, reducing the costs of health care for individuals, and offering the same rates regardless of preexisting conditions—indeed praiseworthy objectives. What is less well known, or less publicized, is the role that the health care industry played behind the scenes and what this means for the quality of health care offered

In the fall of 2008, representatives of the entire health care industry—pharmaceutical manufacturers, insurers, doctors, hospitals, and others—began holding regular meetings with key staff on Capitol Hill. Ted Kennedy and later Max Baucus, the two senators leading the discussions, declared they hoped to come up with a consensus version that at least some of the industries could live with, if not support outright. And this logic of affairs continued under Obama's presidency.[14]

In August 2013 the *Huffington Post* revealed an internal memo that, according to a knowledgeable health care lobbyist, was prepared by a person directly involved in the negotiations.[15] It lists what the White House gave up and what it got in return.

The memo indicates the commitment on the part of the Pharmaceutical Manufacturers and Researchers of America (PhRMA) of up to $80 billion of supposed savings for the consumers. In the memo, key steps in reaching the targeted $80 million concessions were:

1. Agree to increase of Medicaid rebate from 15.1 to 23.1% ($34 billion)
2. Agree to get FOBs [follow-on biological drugs] done (but no agreement on details) ($9 billion)
3. Sell drugs to patients in the donut hole [the gap in coverage for seniors who opt for Medicare drug coverage] at 50% discount ($25 billion)
   This totals $68 billion
4. Companies will be assessed a tax or fee that will score at $12 billion. There was no agreement as to how or on what this tax/fee will be based.
   Total: $80 billion

In exchange for these items, the administration tacitly agreed to do the following, according to the memo:

1. Oppose importation of drugs [from countries that manufacture them more cheaply—e.g., Canada]
2. Oppose rebates in Medicare Part D
3. Oppose repeal of noninterference
4. Oppose opening Medicare Part B [shifting some drugs from Medicare Part B to Medicare Part D, which would cause significant earning losses for pharmaceutical companies]

To reach the landmark ACA reform, five committees held hearings on the issue. The key arbiter of the proposed legislation was the Senate Finance Committee, in which sat many lawmakers with close ties to the health and insurance industries, people who received major campaign contributions. Among the most outspoken supporters of the bill was the already-mentioned Democratic senator Max Baucus.

Let us look more closely at the activities of Max Baucus and his circles. In 2008 Baucus received $1,148,775 from the health sector and $285,850 from the insurance sector. During his career to that point, he had received $2,797,381 from the health sector and $1,170,313 from the insurance sector. Five of Baucus's former staffers worked at the time for a total of twenty-seven different organizations in the health care or insurance sector or for companies directly invested in the outcome of the legislation. Among the twenty-seven were PhRMA, America's Health Insurance Plans (AHIP), Amgen, and GE Health Care.[16] Keep in mind that Senator Baucus has been only one of the many players in this issue.

The whole of the present political conversation turns around continued attempts to repeal so-called Obamacare, and little attention is devoted to how health itself should be defined and what goals should be pursued within a vision of health. The health care reform law was primarily inspired by business, serving corporations first and citizens second. In fact, no bodies of physicians nor the public at large have been consulted in any meaningful way to come up with solutions to a still-looming crisis.

A closer look at the data reveals that the problems with American health care are systemic. A great part of the staggering budget absorbed by health care addresses diseases that affect a small percentage of the population and that are both well-known and conditioned by poor behavioral choices. Consider that 80 percent of the expenses cover too much smoking, eating, drinking, and stress and not enough exercise. Some $30 billion per year is used up by 600,000 people having heart coronary-artery bypasses and 1,300,000 having angioplasties (a technique that mechanically widens narrowed or obstructed arteries). Dr. Edward Miller of Johns Hopkins University indicates, "About half of the bypass grafts clog up in a few years; the angioplasties in a few months." What could be easily addressed by lifestyle becomes a lost opportunity; 90 percent of people having received bypasses have not changed their lifestyle two years after their operations.[17]

Although the political discourse continues to cover fundamental issues in marginally relevant ways, it is clear that the economic sector and private interests have hijacked an eminently universal human concern. Whether we support or oppose Obamacare does not alter the reality of its premises: a health care system dominated by big-business interests.

Health care legislation is hotly debated on both sides of the political divide while the deeper issues lie obscured by the heat of polarized public opinion. Beyond the continuation or repeal of the Affordable Care Act, the cultural dimension of health is simply forgotten. What kind of preventive medicine is good medicine? How do we promote general health and well-being rather than address the costs of poor habits and promote expensive medicines of marginal benefit? Last but not least, the choice of models of medicine has all but been buried. The whole Affordable Care Act presupposes the mechanistic model of the human body and the almost exclusive recourse to allopathic medicine. A whole range of holistic and much more affordable approaches to health care are simply beyond the pale.

For those who suppose that things stand differently in education itself, a closer look will confirm a disheartening reality.

Education under the Corporate Model

The growing alliance between government and big business cannot tolerate a debate on deeper societal questions. Choices on health care

are primarily addressed from the health care industry's end, hardly from medical practitioners' or patients' end of things. The same is true when we enter the most important cultural pursuit of our nation: the education of the next generations.

In 1981 the National Commission on Excellence in Education was established under Reagan to assess the state of American education and propose solutions. In 1983 the report *A Nation at Risk: The Imperative of Educational Reform* spelled out the need to advance new legislation. The report read in part, "If only to keep and improve on the slim competitive edge we still retain in world markets, we must dedicate ourselves to the reform of our educational system for the benefit of all."[18]

In 1989 a first educational summit took place in Virginia, gathering President George Bush and fifty state governors. They agreed to six national goals. One of the goals stated, "US students will be first in the world in science and mathematics achievement." Another one indicated that "every adult in America will be literate and will possess the knowledge and skills necessary to compete in a global economy and exercise the rights and responsibilities of citizenship."[19]

None of the goals that were set for the year 2000 have been met.

The idea of national testing also emerged under the presidency of Bush. He established the New American Schools Development Corporation (NASDC) to spur business leaders to take a leading role in school reform. The challenge was taken up by the national Business Roundtable (BRT), which gathers some 150 CEOs of major corporations in America. The BRT took a leading role in NASDC and outlined nine essential components for educational reform, among which were standards, assessment, accountability, an emphasis on technology in the classroom, and learning readiness. Business leaders emphasized an "outcome-based education" with behavioristic reinforcement techniques. In essence, big business wanted to set the goals and leave freedom to teachers on how to enforce them. Teachers would relinquish all say in the direction that education would take.

After the senior Bush's presidency, there was unanimous agreement across party lines that education would center around national goals, standards, and testing and that business would play a key role in setting the direction of it all. This was given a major impulse under President

Clinton in the formulation of Goals 2000: Educate America Act. The document included eight goals. Among these were a push for "high academic and occupational skill standards," "student performance standards and strategies that all students will be expected to achieve," and "standards that all state and local educational agencies and schools should achieve." Another keystone that has impacted education since was "promoting the use of technology to enable all students to achieve the National Educational Goals."[20] The term "voluntary" was used throughout the document, no doubt because the Constitution does not award Congress power over education. But as a matter of fact, we are seeing the federal government taking complete control over K–12 education.

Seven years after the first national summit, a second summit took place in March 1996 at the IBM conference center in Palisades, New York. It was convened by Tommy G. Thompson, governor of Wisconsin, and Louis V. Gerstner, CEO of IBM and member of BRT. Naturally, Gerstner played a leading role in promoting technology in the classroom. The governors of each state had themselves been encouraged to invite a leading CEO of their states to participate in the summit. Governors and CEOs, in the absence of any educator, advocated for "the development and establishment of academic standards, assessments to measure academic achievement and accountability systems in our states, according to each state's governing structure, within the next two years."[21]

An immediate outcome of the conference was the creation of Achieve, Inc., as a resource center to the states on the key concerns of standards, assessments, accountability, and technology. The two instigators of the conference were also cochairs of the new organization.

Up to this point, government and corporations had taken on education reform, and no input had been requested from or given by educators themselves. Parents and educators were only invited after the two years of recommended implementation of the 1996 summit, at the third educational summit in 1999, which once again took place at the IBM conference center in Palisades, New York, in 1999. This time the event was sponsored by Achieve, Inc; among the cosponsors were the BRT, other business networks, and a number of educational organizations. Educators were invited in the proportion of one per state at a point when their role was simply to enforce previous decisions. In a candid manner, Tommy G. Thompson pointed out that the states had little choice about whether they would go along or not and that the consequences of resisting this change would be drastic. In his words, "but the consequences for the state that doesn't hang in there are even more severe [than those of the students who don't]." The first and most obvious consequence would be being cut off from federal funding.[22]

There was a fourth national education summit in 2001, once again in Palisades. At this summit it was agreed that curriculum would be tied to academic standards and that the delivery of education would be intimately tied to standards and tests. "While the quality of tests is important, the data they provide schools and the public is also vital. Tests must shape instruction by using standards as targets. Simply put, the standards are the North Star of our efforts to improve schools." [23] This long-term vision would affect teacher training, admission to colleges, scholarships, and job placements. And testing would cover all subjects and skills that the state deemed worthy.

Clinton passed the baton to the second President Bush, who signed the 2002 No Child Left Behind Act. This was heavily lobbied for by big business through the Business Coalition for Excellence in Education, under whose umbrella acted seventy national business associations and US corporations. The BRT publicly hailed the success, the part that the coalition played in it, and the fact that most of its recommendations were now the law of the land.[24] Among other things, the NCLB Act required testing for grades 3 to 8, stringent state evaluation of teachers, and a system for rewarding or penalizing schools that did not meet adequate yearly progress (AYP).

In essence, the direction of the school system was to resemble more closely than ever that of a well-run business, within an ideology of global market economy, profit motive, economic competition, and the imperative of economic growth, concludes Gary Lamb, who has thoroughly studied American educational reform.[25] The whole system would evolve toward national teaching standards linked to national curriculum standards, and teachers would be placed on a pay-per-performance salary system, with the public media actively advocating the notion that good education rested on the basis of national standards achieved through high national test scores.

It is no secret that present political power is captive to economic and financial interests. Our inquiry has shown only some major cases. What is happening in politics itself spells out the conditions for a sudden acceleration of big-business impact on all democratic, cultural, and social issues of the immediate future. Government will simply be a more and more docile tool for the dictates of corporations and major financial institutions.

The Ubiquitous Alliance of Government and Corporations: Citizens United

In its 2010 *Citizens United* decision, the Supreme Court effectively allowed unlimited political spending by corporations and unions, leading to an exponential increase in outside spending in elections. Legislators who are targeted by massive outside spending now advocate for more direct contributions for their reelection campaigns to counter the influence of outside spending. And eight states have raised the ceiling for direct individual donations to candidates, and other states are planning to follow suit.[26] So-called dark money groups have devised elaborate ways to fund their causes while concealing their donor sources, encouraging more donations.

Some of the immediate consequences? In the 2008 election, Barack Obama and John McCain combined to spend roughly $1 billion, which was unprecedented. In the same year, spending by candidates, political parties, and interest groups in the congressional and presidential races amounted to combined expenditures of $5.3 billion.[27] That was 2008. Spending through January 21, 2014, was already almost the treble of the corresponding lapse of time in the 2010 election and twenty-five times more than during the 2006 election during the same dates.[28]

The epochal *Citizens United* has resulted in massive amounts of donations moving into shady nonprofit political entities, which are not required to disclose their donors. By 2012 this amount had reached over $300 million, or almost five times what it had been four years before.

Finally, donor disclosure has dropped vertiginously since 2004, from almost 100 percent to just about 40 percent. The remaining 60 percent is shared in equal proportions by groups requiring some disclosure and others requiring none.[29]

Listening for a Different Future

We live in times of increasingly complex issues that are difficult to encompass in their totality. Such problems, added to each other, spell out the conditions for systemic collapse. Representative democracy as it is presently practiced more often than not gathers the fruit of common foolishness, rather than collective intelligence and wisdom. The power of money and corporate interests in the system completely clouds the reality of the issues and controls the way information is spread. Growing polarization among experts and the public adds to the equation; it serves to cover the reality of the issues, as has been shown for health care and education. The result is short-term thinking that only compounds the initial problems.

This book looks at what best ideas are emerging in America from visionaries who are willing to launch forward toward new horizons, leaving behind the moorings of the past. Ideologies tied to political parties or to preferred utopias have had free rein for over a century, promising us new and freer horizons. We are living now in the reality of what they promised us. It is only new thinking, based on more sober apprehension of reality, that can lead us forward. In the pages that follow, we will explore the best that American visionaries have wrought from the jaws of despair. Their contributions rest quite simply on the courage to look at facts without favorite lenses of interpretation and put ideas to the litmus test of reality.

Chapter 2

The Rebirth of Individual Freedom

The world has never had a good definition of the word liberty, and the American people, just now, are much in want of one. We all declare for liberty; but in using the same word we do not all mean the same thing.
—Abraham Lincoln

*I*ndividual freedoms have long been a bedrock of American culture, and they have undergone endless debate in judicial review. In cultural folklore, America continues to be "the land of the free" and the land of "life, liberty and the pursuit of happiness." Yet it can be argued that individual freedoms are often closer to a slogan than to an articulate vision. Under "freedom" can be lumped rights and prerogatives that are at odds with each other and that undermine the universal value of the very freedom they champion. The right to keep and bear arms, sanctioned by the second amendment, when carried to the extreme, could mean license to kill and very little protection for life. Freedom in the sense of the free market means license to pass on the cost of doing business from corporations to taxpayers, who are then deprived of their rights to a clean environment.

It is clear that freedom can be understood only in relation to the human being and its sovereign value. It can be supported only by a generous and encompassing understanding of who we are as human beings and individuals. Ultimately, freedom is not an arbitrary license to do what the individual wants; it is the actualizing of the inner potential of being from the fountain-spring of the self, rather than from prevailing fashions or creeds. It is what upholds the kernel of individuality regardless of race, creed, cultural choices, personal lifestyle, and so on. Only upon this understanding can we build the whole edifice of equality under the law and justice in the political system. It is the present vagueness around the idea of individual freedoms that fosters the inequities in big government and big business.

Freedom and Individuality

In *Legends and Stories for a Compassionate America*, I traced a continuity of development in American culture beginning with George Washington and moving from him to Abraham Lincoln and on to Martin Luther King Jr. These three individuals appeared at critical turning points in the life of the nation, each contributing an important piece of the national identity, forging American values, and reminding us of the power of one that lies in every individual to mold society. Such historical figures deserve a place in the collective memory of a nation. If we survey history across the centuries, from one of these individuals to the next, we see that there is more than meets the eye; each individual was conscious of continuing the work of the one who preceded him or her.

In George Washington the quest for meaning took the form of very earnest participation in the life of Freemasonry and also manifested in his devoted life of prayer. The strength of Washington's inner life played a major role in Valley Forge, when the state of the future nation lay in the balance. A revelation was vouchsafed to him about the future of America, which strengthened his resolve and guided him in the struggle for independence.[1]

It is not surprising, given his moral and spiritual life, that Washington had the strength and future-mindedness to use power with restraint and return to the simple life of the citizen once his office was accomplished. None but Giuseppe Garibaldi and Washington, in their time, had resisted the temptation of absolute power, which lay within reach. Such a thing is common in the third millennium, and contemporaries hardly stop to consider the strength it takes to resist the temptation of power—what it takes now, but even more so, what it took in a time when that power was taken for granted. It was such an example that sustained the nation on a new historical course.

In his early youth, Lincoln read Parson Weems's *Life of Washington*.

Although modern scholarship might view that book as a piece of folklore, it guided Lincoln to a lifelong interest in the first president. In later years, Lincoln would often invoke Washington's name and example, as in a speech to the Young Men's Lyceum in 1838; in his talk to the Temperance Society in 1842; and during the presidency, when he referred to Washington's order to the army to support the Sunday observance (November 5, 1862). Before leaving for the White House, Lincoln prophetically foretold, "Today I leave you; I go to assume a task more difficult than that which devolved upon General Washington. Unless the great God who assisted him shall be with and aid me, I must fail. But if the same omniscient mind and the same Almighty arm that directed and protected him shall guide me and support me, I shall not fail; I shall succeed."[2] In response to a peace petition by a Baltimore resident at the beginning of the Civil War, Lincoln replied, "There is no Washington in that … no manhood nor honor in that."[3] In addition, there are similarities of character between the two great men. Like the first president, Lincoln brought into his cabinet men of diverging, even opposing views. As Washington did, Lincoln could harmonize what could have been unmitigated conflict, all with relative ease.

Beyond these links across the centuries, careful observation reveals that each of these three personalities was devoted to a lifelong quest for the spirit. Lincoln's spiritual life was the more subtle of the three, so much so that it may be ignored, especially if it is convenient for the historian's viewpoint. Denial of this aspect can rest on the unique precedent of Lincoln's refusal to become a member of any particular church, because of his profound mistrust of denominations that would fight each other for the primacy of their revelation. This refusal placed Lincoln above the concerns of Christians of the time, not below; his was a larger view, and his words confirm it in many ways. An example: to Isaac Cogdal, Lincoln spoke on the matter of divine punishment, explaining, according to Cogdal, that "he understood punishment for sin to be a Bible doctrine; that the punishment was parental in its object, aim, and design, and intended for the good of the offender; hence it must cease when justice is satisfied."[4]

Lincoln's interest in the life of the spirit was no passing fancy. To W. H. Crook, a White House guard, Lincoln said, "There are no accidents in my philosophy." He added that cause and effect "are links in the endless chain stretching from the finite to the infinite."[5] Likewise, to a group of ministers in 1862, he commented, "I am conscious every moment that all I am and all I have is subject to the control of a Higher Power."[6]

Nor was Lincoln shy about prayer. He would commend friends to God's care and ask for prayers for himself. John Nicolay confirms that Lincoln prayed and requested the prayers of others. To his friend and journalist Noah Brooks, Lincoln reaffirmed, "I have been driven many times upon my knees by the overwhelming conviction that I had nowhere else to go."[7]

As early as 1842, Lincoln showed his profound knowledge of the Bible and his thoroughly individualized grasp of it. "In regard to this Great Book I have but to say, it is the best gift God has given to man. All the good the Saviour gave to the world was communicated through this book. But for it we could not know right from wrong. All things most desirable for man's welfare, here and hereafter, are to be found portrayed in it."[8] Lincoln's second inaugural address alone has four direct quotations from Genesis, Psalms, and Matthew and another ten allusions to scriptural teachings.[9] Thus, the president who was little prone to public displays of piety nevertheless maintained a quiet and private cultivation of spiritual matters.

What was said of Washington and Lincoln can as well be repeated about Martin Luther King, the only minister of the trio. He carried the spiritual concern in his very vocation. He spoke of the "Beloved Community" and, alone in the civil rights movement, added materialism to the ills of militarism, racism, and imperialism. His views were so universal that he could not operate within the constraints of political alliances and calculations. It was his spiritual commitment alone that allowed him to be a lone voice of conscience for the nation when others, more mindful of the risks, carefully calculated their public stance and statements.

Although all three of these men were deeply connected to the spiritual side of life, they approached it from very personal standpoints. None of them could be confined within the boundaries of a church denomination. They apprehended the spirit in a strictly personal way.

King, although a Baptist, arrived at a formulation of theology that owed much more to his dialectical Hegelian thinking than to creeds. These three towering individuals fulfilled the ideal of individual freedom to the highest degree. They expressed their individuality to the fullest potential. They fostered and promoted the conditions for actualizing the inner potential of being of all Americans from the fountain-spring of the self. American freedom was achieved and expanded through these three outstanding individuals who, not surprisingly, saw themselves as more than the mere product of chance and circumstance, or the offspring of tradition. They were bold innovators who intuited further dimensions of the human condition.

American culture owes these three men an enormous debt of gratitude. Other key individuals also contributed to American culture in the nineteenth and twentieth centuries. They expanded the frontier of consciousness or touched the heads and hearts of many other thinkers, artists, and politicians; enriched popular culture; and recast the nation's collective values. We will look at three of them here: Ralph Waldo Emerson, Bill Wilson, and Elisabeth Kübler-Ross. The latter two are explored in depth in my previous book *A Revolution of Hope*; here only certain themes of their lives and work are presented.[10]

The Power of One: Reasserting the Human

We will now turn our attention to some key individuals who have had a determining impact on American culture. Some of the earlier influences upon culture were examined in *Legends and Stories for a Compassionate America*; among them Benjamin Franklin and Martin Luther King.

Ralph Waldo Emerson

Although the transcendentalist circle was small, many acknowledged a debt of gratitude to Emerson, without necessarily adhering to his entire philosophy. In essence, the transcendentalists were a first expression of an independent spiritual movement centered on a renewed course of thinking and on the reawakening of individual intuition. It was a first successful step on the way toward bridging the divide between mind and heart that characterized the nineteenth century.

To understand the unique role of Emerson, it is useful to look at the polarities that developed in the religious movements in the nineteenth century, a century in which the spread of the scientific outlook brought about important changes in human consciousness. Materialistic thinking—the view that reality consists only of matter, and there is no spirit—grew and reached into every area of life. In America, more than elsewhere, a certain restlessness set in, giving birth to its own manifestations through the interaction of organized religion and social activism, which had also been closely intertwined in the previous century.

The tendencies of the eighteenth century toward extremes were heightened in a dramatic way in the nineteenth. Rationalism had its strongest religious embodiment in unitarianism, which was founded in 1825 when it broke off from the Congregational Church. In unitarianism all the philosophical and political ideas of the English and French philosophers were compressed under a religious umbrella. Unitarianism has been called the democracy of religions. Its creed was expressed by Al Channing: "The adoration of goodness, this is religion."[11] Over time, what united the unitarians was their rejection of the dogma of all other faiths. Overall, they had little success in creating an organized structure and following for their rationalistic outlook.

At the same time, a very different religious movement known as the Second Great Awakening was resurfacing through Revivalism. The first wave hit North Carolina, Virginia, and Maryland in 1787; another one spread through Kentucky and Tennessee in 1799. In the 1820s the Great Revival swept through western New York and the Upper Midwest. Numerous other revivals burst out like wildfires throughout the century. Nothing could characterize the dramatic extremes of the new conversion experience better than the exercises—manifestations of physical-emotional outbursts and frenzy. In the jerking exercises, the peak of religious ecstasy was reached through physical convulsions, sometimes accompanied by outspoken verbalizing. In the barking exercise, people would drop onto all fours and bark and then run in packs to trees, like dogs treeing an opossum. Many of these physical exercises were meant to induce visions and trances. The French historian Tocqueville, shocked at observing such practices, attributed them to extreme swings between a pronounced materialistic pursuit of welfare and the balancing attempt to satisfy the soul's hunger for spiritual experience.[12] His observation was correct; at that time individuals could move with relative ease between the two extremes of evangelism and liberalism.

The changing times accentuated the polarities. Elsewhere this restlessness of mind and will gave way to what we may call a prophetic mood. On a large scale, this foreboding mood became apocalyptic millennialism—a belief in a sort of thousand-year spell of paradise on earth, which would be followed by a final judgment, bringing the physical world to an end. Many of these elements informed the growth of the Millerism movement, which predicted the end of the world by 1844. Although the movement did not have the million followers it claimed, it certainly gained a considerable number, often drawing in famous personalities.

Many reform campaigns appeared in the political arena, closely allied with religious fervor—movements such as temperance, prison reform, improved treatment of the insane, women's rights, and the peace movement. The entire spectrum of religious denominations participated in these pursuits. The formation of utopian communities also came mainly from religious groups. Most successful among them were the Shakers and the Mormons. Even the more sober transcendentalists had their own community at Brook Farm in Massachusetts. The religious and spiritual movements were far more successful than political attempts at utopian communities, which included the North American Phalanx (Pennsylvania and New Jersey); Etienne Cabet's Icaria (Texas); and Robert Owen's New Harmony (Indiana).

Emerson set a high ideal for Americans to reach toward. He considered that Americans should have their eyes toward the entire world, not just America; they should be world citizens, mindful of the fact that many of the world's races and folk were (and continue to be) gathered in America. And he was concerned that most Americans in his time had only material concerns on their minds. In his famous address "The American Scholar," he said, "A nation of men will for the first time exist because each believes himself inspired by the divine soul which also inspires all men."[13]

Being a thinker and a poet, Emerson set his mind to the ambitious goal of recasting the American mind. For that purpose he referred to two kinds of thinking: arithmetical-logical thinking and intuitive thinking. The second, he claimed, belongs more strongly to the will and connects us to the world of the spirit. It is a thinking that needs to be more strongly developed now, rather than the ubiquitous logical head thinking. Head thinking alone leads us to separation because on its own it is incapable of recognizing spiritual reality.

The following words can help us comprehend what he had in mind when he referred to intuitive thinking: "All your progress is an unfolding, like the vegetable bud. You have first an instinct, then an opinion, then a knowledge, as the plant has root, bud, and fruit. Trust the instinct to the end, though you can render no reason. It is vain to hurry it. By trusting it to the end, it shall ripen into truth and you shall know why you believe." And further: "When we consider the people who have stimulated and supported us, we will become aware of the superiority of the spontaneous or intuitive principle over the arithmetic or logical one. The first contained hidden within itself the nature of the second."[14] By "instinct," Emerson meant those universal human drives that call us to the pursuit of truth, beauty, or goodness—everything that lives in the depths of the human psyche and drives it toward self-improvement.

In Emerson's view, we move in stages to reach the height of intuitive thinking, from instincts to spiritual knowledge. In the first stage we discover spiritual instincts that live in our souls (the root). Subsequently, we form an opinion about these instincts, but it is still subjective (the bud). Finally, with effort, we attain a spiritual knowledge, which is no longer subjective (the fruit). Emerson is the living example of what he says here. By trusting his instincts, he saw a new way to reconcile faith and science, to reconcile the religious inspiration he drew from the East with the modern Western way of thinking. His instincts first required that he break his ties with unitarianism and that he seek truth from all the great philosophical traditions and world religions and from the cultural ferment of his time. Only later could he build a cohesive worldview. Along this path, the logical thinking of the West could rise to his concept of intuitive thinking. This formulation could only evolve slowly and unfold like a plant. The poet had to trust his instincts at the time in which they provided him with no more than a distant image, set out on a long quest, and endure long spells of doubt, before acquiring inner certainty.

The transcendentalists were attempting to forge a modern path toward the spirit that would draw from all religious and spiritual traditions without being bound to any. Emerson had resigned from the unitarian ministry dissatisfied. In his approach he denied not only dogma, as the unitarians did, but also rationalism. His circle drew inspiration from German philosophical idealism, literary Romanticism, and the Greek philosophers, among other sources. Emerson had also immersed himself in the sacred texts of world religions, particularly Eastern ones. This vast gamut of inspirational sources shows how much the transcendentalists were experimenters with the inner path.

Emerson was completely inspired by the spirit of his time. He knew that humanity was reaching a new watershed and that new faculties of perception into the spirit would arise. He expressed it in this way: "The indicators of the values of matter are degraded to a sort of cooks and confectioners, on the appearance of the indicators of ideas. Genius is the naturalist or geographer of the supersensible regions, and draws their map; and, by acquainting us with new fields of activity, cools our affection for the old. These are at once accepted as the reality, of which the world we have conversed with is the show."[15]

Emerson was also the herald of a new understanding of the thorny concept of human destiny. He intuited that destiny has its origin within the human being. He sensed that there is a close relationship between the individual and what occurs in the individual's environment. Everything that happens to the individual corresponds to one's inner needs; it fits the purpose of one's inner evolution. With hindsight he could detect that our apparent misfortunes are often exactly what is needed in order for us to enter into new paths in life or acquire skills that could later be indispensable for our most important life pursuits. The human being has shaped his or her destiny in concert with the higher power, and this knowledge will serve to give strength and resolve in life.

The paradox of Emerson's way between East and West is what the poet Oliver Wendell Holmes captured in his description of Emerson, in the poem "At the Saturday Club": "Where in the realm of thoughts, whose air is song, does he the Buddha of the West, belong? He seems a Franklin, sweetly wise, born to unlock the secrets of the skies."

Emerson added important building blocks to the edifice of freedom. He further detached the individual from dogma and tradition, without rendering the individual the victim of environment and circumstance. He traced the outlines for a thoroughly individual quest for meaning and an individually based morality. He freed the individual from the dogmas of tradition, religious or scientific, without throwing him into the abyss of the growing materialism of the times.

Bill Wilson and the Twelve-Step Program

Taking a leap from the nineteenth into the twentieth century, we explore a new phenomenon inspired by a different personality. Now we look at an individuality diametrically opposed to Emerson's: that of Bill Wilson, the founder of Alcoholics Anonymous and father of the recovery movement. Though Wilson contributed to his culture through raw willpower, and Emerson was a master of intellectual argument and inspiration, both expanded the understanding of what it means to be an individual in our time and therefore rendered the pursuit of freedom more meaningful.

Bill Wilson, born thirteen years after Emerson's death, was a man of uncommon abilities. In his school years he excelled not only academically but also artistically and athletically. He played the first violin in the orchestra and was captain of the baseball team. Many other achievements could be listed. Nevertheless, he became an alcoholic, and his contribution to American culture was completed only after a long journey through a personal abyss. This path of transformation was marked by two key epiphanies.

The first spiritual experience came to Wilson when he was visiting Winchester cathedral during World War I. Remembering this earlier experience, he described having felt ecstasy and having been stirred by a "tremendous sense of presence." He wrote, "For a brief moment, I had needed and wanted God. There had been a humble willingness to have Him with me—and He came."[16] Soon after, Wilson found himself reading the epitaph of a young man who had died from alcohol at age twenty-six. This was the perfect warning and call to a new life:

Here lies a Hampshire grenadier,
Who caught his death
Drinking cold small beer.
A good soldier is ne'er forgot,
Whether he dieth by musket
Or by pot.[17]

The ambitious young Wilson was not particularly inclined toward religion or the spiritual at that point in his life. The Winchester experience and the accompanying warning from the epitaph were not sufficient as incentives or as deterrents to the life experiences that followed. Bill Wilson continued to drink, and his health only deteriorated. In 1933 he entered Towns Hospital in New York City, where he met the remarkable Dr. W. D. Silkworth. Wilson later returned to the hospital a second time, realizing that he could not get rid of his torments. He was now enduring constant physical and emotional torture and depression, suffering continuous hallucinations, and contemplating suicide.

By 1934, Dr. Silkworth was concerned about Wilson's health and sanity. A new constellation of events had set in, however. Wilson had been touched by the testimonial of his friend Ebby, who had renounced alcohol through religion. Wilson felt remorse for his behavior toward his wife, and he now recalled the Winchester cathedral experience. In anguish, and believing this was his end, he found himself kneeling, crying out to God, "I'll do anything, anything at all!" In the experience that followed, Bill felt the room blazing with indescribably white light. In ecstasy, he was standing upon a summit, wind blowing through him, a thought crossing his mind: "You are a free man!" After the ecstasy, consciousness of his surroundings returned. He now felt a presence, like a sea of living spirit. "Even though a pilgrim upon an uncertain highway, I need be concerned no more, for I had glimpsed the great beyond."[18] Wilson, who had just turned thirty-nine, no longer doubted the work of the spirit; nor did he ever take another drink.

Another important step was needed before personal experience could turn into guiding the collective recovery of hundreds and thousands. In 1935, after losing the opportunity to become a financial officer in the National Rubber Machinery Company in Akron, Ohio, Wilson found himself alone in the town. His mind was reeling again next to the abyss, longing for quick escape. The thought hit him that he needed to talk to another recovering alcoholic; from one contact to another, he was finally put in touch with a Dr. Robert Smith. After a conversation that continued overnight and into the morning hours, the two men started immediately to work with other alcoholics, founding Alcoholics Anonymous (AA) and the famous twelve-step program.

Wilson continued a lifelong search for answers, looking at matters such as reincarnation and spiritualism and seeking answers in Catholicism. He could not easily accept dogma, even though he recommended that AA recovering members join a church and was himself friend with many clergymen. Wilson realized that both science and religion had a vested interest in life after death and that both argued for blind faith, either against or in favor of immortality. Neither could accommodate much free inquiry and debate on the matter. His rather unconventional beliefs can be seen in the following quote: "Everything considered, I felt that proof of survival [after death] would be one of the greatest events that could take place in the Western world today. It wouldn't necessarily make people good. But at least they could really know what God's plan is, as Christ so perfectly demonstrated at Easter time. Easter would become a fact; people could then live in a universe that would make sense."[19] Though nowhere articulated as a conceptually coherent worldview, spirituality lives nevertheless in the path that Wilson received through inspiration and that he transmitted to alcoholics, and later to people suffering from any and all kind of dependency.

The twelve steps are worth repeating here for those who may not know them in detail.

Step 1: We admitted we were powerless over alcohol—that our lives had become unmanageable.

Step 2: Came to believe that a Power greater than ourselves could restore us to sanity.

Step 3: Made a decision to turn our will and our lives to the care of God as we understood him.

Step 4: Made a searching and fearless moral inventory of ourselves.

Step 5: Admitted to God, ourselves, and to another human being the exact nature of our wrongs.

Step 6: Were entirely ready to have God remove all these defects of character.

Step 7: Humbly asked him to remove our shortcomings.

Step 8: Made a list of all persons we harmed, and became willing to make amends to them all.

Step 9: Made direct amends to such people wherever possible, except when to do so would injure them or others.

Step 10: Continued to take personal inventory, and when we were wrong promptly admitted it.

Step 11: Sought through prayer and meditation to improve our conscious contact with God as we understood Him, praying only for knowledge of His will for us and the power to carry it out.

Step 12: Having had a spiritual awakening as the result of these steps, we tried to carry the message to alcoholics, and to practice these principles in all our affairs.[20]

The life of alcoholics or addicts is an endless, repetitive act of denial of reality. Initiating the twelve-step process means being willing to acknowledge our powerlessness and open up to the idea of a higher power (steps 1 to 3). This is just the first breach in the armor that surrounds addicts and that nullifies all their well-meaning efforts. It concerns the intellect. A second significant step comes when individuals make a moral inventory with an open heart and let themselves be touched in their feelings through an understanding of the pain they have caused to others (steps 4 to 7). They thereby acquire new faculties of empathy. Finally, in steps 8 and 9, the candidates jump into the crucible of the transformation of the will, when they go through the zero point of making themselves completely vulnerable and powerless and make amends to all those they have hurt. This is truly a turning point, a place of seeming void that opens new doors. Past and future meet in the willingness to make oneself truly powerless; but new, deeper power emerges that connects individuals with their higher selves and with what the future is calling them to become.

In all the successive stages, the individual goes from being supported by the organization to becoming an active supporter and shaper. At step 10, what has been gained from the previous stages becomes an ongoing practice. This is what allows the point of openness to the future to become a source of continuous inspiration. The individual experiences the stage of openness to the future not just once, but must return to it over and over again. Step 11 means fully taking responsibility for our lives and being able to carry others; part of this is taking up an active discipline of prayer and/or meditation. The recovering addicts are now putting their shoulders to the wheel, so to speak, not only for personal recovery but also for the good of the group, and eventually the good of the twelve-step programs itself. Finally, step 12 means complete dedication to and adoption in daily life of the goals of the twelve-step process, which means contributing to the continuance and regeneration of twelve-step itself.

Not surprisingly, from the accrued effects of all these steps practiced by thousands of individuals over many decades, not only is AA effective in its group work, but it is also very innovative, solid, and efficient in its organizational structure. The benefits of the group approach have been recognized and used by countless other groups, many of which have little or no connection to alcohol addiction (see Sidebar 2.1).

What began as a challenge for survival—individuals' dependency on alcohol—marked one of the most significant revolutions in the way of looking at the individual in America. The twelve-step program showed the way to the recovery of individuality previously blotted out by the scourge of alcoholism. It paved the way from *spiritus* (Latin for alcohol) to true spirit, by showing that a precious divine spark was still and always present, even in the most desperate of alcoholics. It showed, not in words or concepts, but in action and results, the power that individuality and dogma-free group consciousness could achieve over and against all odds. It prevailed where religious doctrine or modern science could not. That strength, which an individual displays when he or she stands at the edge of the abyss, is the epitome of human freedom.

SIDEBAR 2.1: Growth of Twelve-Step Programs

1957: Al-Anon Family Groups, fellowship of relatives and friends of alcoholics
1957: Gamblers Anonymous (GA)
1960: Overeaters Anonymous (OA)
1964: Neurotics Anonymous (a predecessor of Emotions Anonymous)
1968: Debtors Anonymous (DA)
1971: Families Anonymous (FA) for relatives and friends of addicts
1977: Sex Addicts Anonymous (SAA)
1982: Cocaine Anonymous (CA)
1982: Survivors of Incest Anonymous (SIA)
1986: Co-Dependents Anonymous (CoDA)
1986: Nicotine Anonymous (NicA)
1987: Food Addicts Anonymous
1989: Emotions Anonymous (EA)
1994: Crystal Meth Anonymous (CMA)
2008: On-Line Gamers Anonymous (OLGA)

Elisabeth Kübler-Ross

It may cause some surprise that Elisabeth Kübler-Ross is included among our roster of American cultural pioneers. She is the person who did the most to revolutionize the care of the dying in this country through hospice. Kübler-Ross was a physician, born and trained in Switzerland, a land of staunch traditions, but America offered her the opportunity to innovate. This is how she viewed the contrast: "My destiny had to be the United States, where I was free to pursue my own work, my own research, and my own teaching, none of which could have been possible in any other part of the world."[21]

Kübler-Ross was in the unique situation of witnessing the contrast between the way an old culture made death part of life and the American antithesis—a society where death was shunned and completely ignored. Another element prepared Kübler-Ross to be a trailblazer in her field. Although deeply steeped in tradition, her family was not religious. When she met the scientific worldview, she naturally adopted it, while at the same time retaining everything she had been taught during her upbringing. All her spiritual yearnings could not be blotted out by her scientific knowledge, and later she did actively pursue a spiritual understanding of the world.

At age twenty-one, Kübler-Ross met a woman whom she called Golda, who had been in the concentration camp of Maidanek, Poland. Golda, a German Jew—a miraculous survivor of the gas chambers—had undergone a complete spiritual rebirth. Although the rest of Golda's family had been killed, she had vowed to forgive all who caused her hurt. Because of the contrast between the horror of Maidanek and Golda's love, Kübler-Ross formulated important questions that would determine the later course of her life: How can evil hold sway in the world in such a way? How can individuals allow it to happen?

Another question came to her from the American medical profession's attitude toward dying patients. Why was death ignored and shunned? Why were dying people left with no support? These questions led her to explore the experience of dying people, first by simply listening to them. Later she came to understand ways to alleviate their suffering.

In 1969, when she was forty-three, two important events propelled her to the task that made her famous. The Macmillan Publishing Company asked her to write 50,000 words on death and dying; the resulting book, *On Death and Dying*, sold very well. In that same year, *Life* magazine published the famous article about Kübler-Ross's interview with Eva—a twenty-one-year-old woman dying of leukemia. From the reaction of her colleagues at the hospital of Northwestern University Medical Center of Chicago, Kübler-Ross knew she could not continue her work in the same setting or within the scientific community. The reaction to her book, and the immediate responses of readers to the *Life* article, propelled her into a new career—offering workshops about death and dying all around the world.

What may easily be overlooked about Kübler-Ross is the place that her own spiritual experiences held for her and the impact this had on her questions about death. In a revealing statement in her autobiography, she said, "If I had not been on the other side, I would not be able to be with dying children, with parents of murdered children."[22]

Kübler-Ross had at least three other important spiritual experiences. The first occurred in 1976, at the Monroe Farm in Virginia. This was a laboratory environment designed to stimulate out-of-body experiences. She was in a soundproof booth, lying on a waterbed, eyes blindfolded. Relaxation was induced by artificial sound pulses. Against the advice of the scientists, she asked that they send the highest impulses possible. She said of the resulting experience that she did not know where she was, and she had the feeling of having gone too far. When she went to sleep, she was besieged by nightmares, and she said it was like going through a thousand deaths. She experienced—bodily and psychologically—the deaths of all the patients she had assisted, one after the other. The pain was so intense that she somehow got to the other side, rising above it. After a series of experiences connected with the perception of her body as an energetic field, she came into contact with the white light that she knew from the descriptions of her dying patients, and she merged into a blissful state of warmth and love. On first coming out of the experience in a heightened state, she could perceive the energetic field of all living beings. When that state faded, she then had to struggle to reintegrate herself into everyday life and the apparently humdrum nature of everyday reality.

A second experience, which occurred two years later, was a typical near-death experience (NDE) caused by three bites of black widow spiders. Kübler-Ross felt she had a choice between living and dying; she made a vow to keep living. At that moment she felt enveloped by a bright light and moved toward it, knowing that she would survive.

A final NDE occurred when she visited her sister Eva in Switzerland in 1988. There she expressed to Eva that she was dying and ready to go. Once again, she experienced the white light and returned to this side of existence.

In many ways Kübler-Ross was endowed with special gifts of perception. One of those she described as follows:

I have had the great blessing of being able to see with my own physical eyes the presence of hundreds of those energy patterns [of people] in full daylight. And it is very similar to a fluttering, pulsating series of different snowflakes, all with their different lights and colors and their different forms and shapes. This is what we look like after we die. This is also how we exist before we are born. We take up no space and it takes us no time to go from one star to another or from planet Earth to another galaxy.[23]

These observations undoubtedly point to Kübler-Ross's special mission in connection to death and dying. In her, we find the desire of the modern soul to bring spirituality and science into a dialogue where neither is subjugated to the other. (See Sidebar 2.2.)

The results of Kübler-Ross's life task echo what we have heard in relation to Emerson and Bill Wilson. Not only did the doctor challenge science's limits; she herself experienced what lay beyond those limits, having a firsthand experience—no matter how limited—of what is considered the domain of religion. She was both the investigator and the object of her studies. And she conducted her work while pursuing, as much as she knew and could, the scientific paradigm that she had espoused as a student of medicine. If the kernel of individuality survives death, then it is in this immortal seed that a power transcending genetic and environmental determinism lies. Individuality is the very expression and heart of human freedom, and it lives equally in all human beings. Kübler-Ross could also perceive spiritually this kernel and see that it expresses itself uniquely in every person.

SIDEBAR 2.2: Milestones in the Growth of Hospice in the United States

1967: St. Christopher's Hospice is founded by Cicely Saunders in South London.

1968: Florence Wald, dean of Yale School of Nursing, spends a year at St. Christopher.

1969: Elisabeth Kübler-Ross publishes *On Death and Dying*, which becomes an international best seller.

1972: Kübler-Ross speaks on the subject of death and dying, from hospice's perspective, at national hearings held by the US Senate Special Committee on Aging.

1974: Connecticut Hospice (in Branford, CT), the first American hospice, is founded by Florence Wald, two pediatricians, and a chaplain.

1974: Senators Frank Church and Frank E. Moss introduce the first, though unsuccessful, legislation for granting federal funds to hospice programs.

1979: Demonstration programs in twenty-six US hospice facilities, promoted by the Health Care Financing Administration (HCFA), are used to help define hospice and its work and assess its cost-effectiveness.

1993: President Clinton's health care reform proposal allows all Americans to benefit from hospice services.

1996: Considerable amounts of private funds are invested in research, new programs, conferences, and public events to promote the work of hospice and transform public opinion.

2000: The series *On Our Own Terms: Moyers on Dying in America* airs on PBS, in an effort aimed at national education and community action.

2004: US hospices serve more than one million Americans at the end of life.

2005: More than 4,000 hospice provider organizations operate in the United States.

2009: A record 550,000 hospice volunteers operate throughout the country.

(Information abridged and edited from National Hospice and Palliative Care Organization's website, 2014, http://www.nhpco.org/history-hospice-care.)

The Power of Civil Society: Redefining the Social Experience

How could we possibly measure the cumulative impact that souls like Emerson, Wilson, Kübler-Ross, and others have had on American culture? These three pioneers share more than meets the eye. Each pursued an understanding of the spirit that was unique for his or her time. The elder, Emerson, pursued a path in his thinking; Wilson and Kübler-Ross forged ahead through the experience of their life's missions. Emerson had given up his role of minister, which was too constricting for his cultural vision and ideals. Wilson gained firsthand experience of the spiritual dimension of the human experience, with which he confronted the scourge of alcohol. Kübler-Ross did the same in confronting the inevitability of death. All three fought to find spiritual meaning in a culture that denied it—the culture of scientific materialism. But they did not accept answers from a tradition of religious dogma either. They found hope at the bottom of the abyss. Emerson faced the abyss of meaninglessness in culture. Religion could no longer give him the answers he needed. Bill Wilson faced the way society had turned its back on the spirit, seeking to find its replacement in King Spiritus—alcohol. Kübler-Ross faced the materialistic denial of life beyond death, which she could do only because she gained a firsthand perspective from the other side.

Emerson is no doubt the American philosopher who has most inspired many generations of thinkers and visionaries. His thoughts freed religious, spiritual, and scientific investigations from the shackles of dogma and tradition. He intuited the last frontier that defines the domain of culture: "[the genius] appears as an exponent of vaster mind and will. The opaque self becomes transparent with the light of the First Cause."[24]

The work of Wilson and Kübler-Ross, the other two pioneers who lived nearer to our time, can also be assessed. All we need to do is look around at the social landscape, as it has been affected by the work of hospice and the twelve-step programs. To those who were born in the 1940s or 1950s, it is undeniable that a quiet revolution has occurred in the perception of the matter of dying. We have now moved into an age when the question of death has evolved from a subject that was shunned or completely taboo to a large open horizon for exploration, with innumerable books, workshops, and conferences available. At least for many, it is clear that death is no longer the final threshold, the end, the period in a sentence. Granted, this new journey is only beginning, but it is one that many now embark upon.

On another front, the work of the twelve-step programs ultimately addresses the question of what it means to be a human being, the question around which all of culture moves. Through the journey that is conveniently divided into twelve steps, the candidate for recovery learns to see himself as the arena of a battle between inner light and darkness; a candidate learns to contemplate herself not only as an all-too-earthly human being but also as a spiritual entity. Wilson himself used to say that our life on earth is a "mere day in a school" and that we are all "pupils in a spiritual kindergarten."[25]

Recovery is possible only when the former addict connects with a higher power that he did not wish or did not know how to consider before. The twelve-step programs show us that we are more than earthly beings; we are individual spiritual essences. It is through reconnection to this truth that we can find a place once more in society. Feeling ourselves to be both earthly and spiritual at the same time causes a tremendous dynamic tension in all of us modern human beings. It is the engine from which culture can derive its impetus. It is not surprising that this dynamic was expressed by both Wilson and Kübler-Ross, from a deep conviction derived from personal experience.

It may be said in passing that nowhere have modern spiritual experiences, such as NDEs, affected as large a number of people as in America. According to the Near-Death Experience Research Foundation (NDERF), 774 NDEs occur every day in the United States.[26] Part of this can be explained by the increased rate of the experiences at the hand of modern medical resuscitation techniques. The phenomenon of NDE that was experienced by Bill Wilson and Elisabeth Kübler-Ross has also been explored by George Ritchie, Dannion Brinkley, Betty Eadie, Rufus Moseley, G. Scott Sparrow, and many others.[27]

The accretion of the work of all of these individuals and the impact their work has had on modern American consciousness are only the beginning of a possible cultural revolution. Only if the disharmony and tension inherent in modern individualism are recognized and embraced can it serve as the stepping-stone for the creation of a new culture. The distance between traditionally held religious values and modern emptiness of soul is the driving engine for a search for meaning. The three cultural heralds we have reviewed invite us to see the human being as much more than the product of chance, genetics, environment, upbringing, and cultural conditioning. These individuals intuited that all human beings can know inner freedom because they are both earthly and spiritual beings.

The twelve-step programs and hospice are but two of the institutions that contribute to the creation of a new culture. They started as the work of two individuals and their cohorts; at present hospice and twelve-step groups form a network that permeates all of American social reality. When we turn our gaze to the larger social field, we can recognize the larger movement that is at work reshaping our culture—the emerging civil society, the social arena of society that is independent from the private (economic) and the public sectors.

America is standing at a fork in the road, along with much of the rest of humanity. Will we perpetually repeat the past, or will we learn from a future that wants to come into being? It is now undeniable that we have to confront problems of new dimensions with openness of mind and sensitivity of heart. When that confrontation happens fully, new doors open, and the unexpected takes place. One such confrontation did happen; it even ushered in the new millennium.

In the United States the new century was welcomed during the so-called Battle of Seattle in 1999. For the first time in American and global history, the agenda of the world economic elite was brought to a halt. The unexpected outcome expressed the power of an emerging force that had never manifested at a global level before: the power of civil society and its constellation of nongovernmental organizations (NGOs).

The American-led push for a global market that disregards culture, labor, and the environment—and in short, everything but the most materialistic human pursuits—received a challenge from the only sector of society that can promote new values: civil society. Before the event at Seattle, only global business and the power of government (and its international extensions in the European Union, NAFTA, CAFTA, WTO, and so forth) had contended for the world stage. In Seattle, fifty thousand demonstrators belonging to a network of national and international NGOs championed ideas of freedom, human rights, respect for the environment, and the rights of indigenous peoples and minorities. This was the first time that NGOs had emerged as a force of their own, rather than delegating their representation to political parties or ideologies.

Civil society organizations are an amorphous conglomerate, often unaware of their own strength, with the potential to promote a third sector that not only stands in contrast with the private (business) and public sectors, but that also can have constructive dialogue with them. Seen at their best, NGOs have the opportunity to fashion a newly independent realm of culture. It is from this sector that the realm of ideas, knowledge, science, arts, and ethics can be defined—not from the economy or from government. It is this arena that sustains human motivation and behavior.

The current dominant economic globalization works from the premise of the primacy of the economy and from the absence of a real culture. It is a universal downward leveler of human values, behavior, and meaning. It is what Benjamin Barber calls a "McWorld," sustained by vague notions of Western tradition but actually defined by absence and vacuum rather than by real presence, substance, and meaning.[28] At the Seattle event, enough people awoke and started to ask what future their society really wanted.

It is through a dialogue that includes government, business, and civil society that we can advance worldwide sustainable development and continue to evolve the cultural/spiritual activism that lay in the visions of Emerson, Wilson, Kübler Ross and others. By allying the strengths of both social movements and consciousness movements, a new culture can propose a paradigm where social change mirrors a deep individual change of consciousness and is sustained from it. Such a change of consciousness is the only thing that can promote a more compassionate future America. Political change alone will not do it.

At present the agenda of elite globalization does much more than map an exploitation of the planet in which all parts fulfill only the role of cogs in a machine. That agenda also determines how financial markets will benefit from unrestricted mobility worldwide, establishes which countries will produce cheap goods for the rest of the world, determines how much labor will cost, and so forth. And these are but surface factors. At a deeper level lies an image of the human being. This brave new world will be populated by human beings deprived of soul and spirit, people who will be able, with indifference, to eat genetically modified or otherwise engineered, synthetic foods; who will repair, enhance, or alter their body functions through nanotechnology; who will extend intellectual and functional capacities through the incorporation of microrobotics and artificial intelligence; who will live their lives in a virtual bubble; and who, in the midst of looming possible world catastrophe, will continue the uninterrupted march toward a future dominated by coal, oil, or nuclear energy. The mechanized image of humanity is at one end of a continuum; at the other end are the fundamentalisms of various streams, which look only at a personal heaven or nirvana detached from any social dimension and which often project outwardly apocalyptic scenarios that claim to bring the beginning of a new era.

Although we may seek to resist mechanization and reification of the planet, if our culture remains materialistic, it will be condemned to repeat the patterns of the past. In the present materialistic mind-set, the concepts of human rights, respect for the environment, and respect for world cultures are little more than good intentions and empty phrases. All of these values and ideas were traditionally held by religion and must now be renewed from sources of the spirit, in the ways in which hospice, twelve-step programs, and other cultural entities are only beginning to do.

Cultural change renders new things possible because it opens the gates of our imagination and creativity. It is through this potent cultural renewal that we will have an extended, mobile, constantly renewable source of leadership. The inspired leadership that Martin Luther King Jr. demonstrated will be found in innumerable individuals with a newly awakened social imagination. The Arab Spring and Occupy Wall Street have shown us what strength lies in ordinary individuals doing extraordinary things because they are truly awake to the needs of the time. Cultural renewal will ultimately redefine the elusive yearning for freedom. Where a new project of society is deeply rooted in a fuller image of the human being, the uniqueness of each individual will shine as a matter of fact. Promoting this individuality through a more holistic education, sustaining it, and removing all obstacles to its expression will be the natural desire of a new culture. As the new culture sustains the freedom of the individual, so does the full expression of individuality offer new contributions to society and strengthen its culture in turn, in what could be called a "virtuous cycle."

It was not economic wealth that made the United States the country of the Declaration of Independence, at a turning point of modern consciousness that was marked by the conquest of the Americas and the development of the scientific outlook. The whole American continent could have birthed social and cultural renewal. Many South American countries had as much wealth as the United States, or more.

It was not a strong political class or a sudden political revolution that made possible the Declaration of Independence or government for and by the people. Such things have been tried elsewhere and have failed. Rather, what made the US federal government possible was the vast arena of a diverse and manifold cultural ferment. Many civic organizations that blossomed in colonial America played a great part in shaping cultural renewal. One example is the civic initiatives generated in Benjamin Franklin's Philadelphia, which gave rise to the Junto, the library, the fire company, and fire insurance.

The life of colonial ideas teemed within a still-vibrant Masonry. No single religion held the nation in its grip. Nor did any particular religion hold a monopoly in any given colony—not Quakerism in Pennsylvania, Catholicism in Maryland, or Congregationalism in New England.

This vibrant exchange of ideas, formation of identity, and forging of meaning was missing in most, if not all, parts of Latin America, from Mexico to Argentina and Chili. Most of these countries have the expanse of territory and the resources that the United States possesses. What they lacked was the cultural aliveness, manifested in cultural pluralism, that offers the basis for societal renewal.[29] It is this cultural renewal that is most urgently needed at present in the United States and worldwide. And the basis for such a radical shift is already present in the work of daring visionaries, as we will see in the next chapters.

Chapter 3

The Evolving Horizon of Equality

Creating the capacity for public wisdom in twenty-first century America is no greater challenge than that faced by our country's original Founders. But this is our task, our calling. We are the revolutionary founders of this new democracy, a democracy that will have an impact at least as great, and probably greater, than the impact their revolution had on the world almost 250 years ago.

—Tom Atlee

A revolution in the way we approach politics is afoot. It has actually been going on for a while. Now, however, it is gaining consciousness of itself, building strength and reaching out for recognition. Democracy by means of the two-party system has served its purpose, even if it were to work at its best. Delegating our voices is but a part of what democracy can be.

Party politics works on a number of assumptions. First and foremost are the ideologies that have given birth to the right and the left. Under whatever modern shades they appear in the present, they are derivations of free market ideology, harking back to Adam Smith, its originator, or forms of socialism, social democracy, liberalism, and so on whose roots can be found in Marxian theory. When two such ideologies meet each other, compromise is unavoidable, and a continuous blending of the two permeates the political reality of the present. Compromise brings with it the belief that only the majorities will find satisfaction, and only for a certain time. More often than not, even majorities themselves will settle for what is possible rather than what they desire.

As we will see later in this chapter, stronger participation in the democratic process can move close to direct democracy. This is possible thanks to the new approaches of dialogue, deliberation, and "social technology," which have been tested at the level of organizations, municipalities, cities, and larger geographical units. Dialogue and deliberation rest on the idea of polling samples of the population that represent all political perspectives and every imaginable level of social demographics in order to formulate recommendations or create policy. Key to this approach is access to as unbiased and diverse sources of information as possible. Closely allied to, and often an integral part of, dialogue and deliberation itself are techniques of facilitation and decision making that we can gather under the name of social technology. Suffice it to say that social technology allows communities or organizations to go through a creative process in which a common will is strengthened and decisions emerge that rest on near consensus. When we move from organizations to the body politic, consensus is no longer sought, but rather, supermajorities.

A new view of democratic participation has made headlines in recent years through Occupy Wall Street and its sister movements. We have seen what look like spontaneous, unorganized, and constantly changing masses build consensus over time in a seemingly unpredictable process. To many the results may have seemed stunning. To those who have followed American social innovation over the last decades, this is but a natural outgrowth of decades of action, research, and experimentation. From twelve-step programs to nonviolent communication to Appreciative Inquiry, World Café, Theory U, consensus decision making, and the numerous expressions of so-called social technology, a whole new way of moving from compromise to wide alliances, and even consensus, has been gaining ground in the last decades. An American body of practice knows how to move complex and highly evolving systems toward outcomes that serve the needs of all constituencies.

The methodologies cited previously address personal, group, and organizational social change in America. They are aimed at the formation of, and they work with, a new group consciousness that comes among people who are working together in harmony, while retaining complete individual freedom.

Twelve-step programs, nonviolent communication, and social technology, as treated in these chapters, are just landmarks; for each example that is offered here, innumerable variations could be presented that offer similar threads. Not only is this landscape very wide; it is also largely unrecognized and underestimated. No comprehensive review or history of these movements has been attempted, to my knowledge.

Processes of Social Transformation: Inspiration from the Past

American social innovation inserts itself in a historical continuum, in a cultural tradition. As asserted in my *Legends and Stories for a Compassionate America*, the Haudenosaunee (Iroquois) cultural revolution was a precursor for the emergence of the American form of government. This watershed event affected two levels of reality: the external political structure known as the Longhouse and another, more subtle inner aspect, which we could call processes of social transformation. The most famous form of the latter was the Ritual of Condolence, which addressed the causes of grief that disturbed the life of the confederacy. Grievances between the tribes, or even within a single tribe, were a threat to the working of the Haudenosaunee. If a tribe mourned the death of one of its own at the hand of another tribe, the common peace was at risk. The Iroquois addressed this problem by healing the root cause of social disturbances before it reached the higher levels of governance. This is why the Ritual of Condolence was an important part of healthy government. It was the way of reconciling individual psychological health with healthy social life. Political structures and social rituals were closely intertwined. We could say that the inner aspect of the cultural revolution historically preceded the creation of the Longhouse. First, Deganawidah performed the Ritual of Condolence for Hiawatha, and then together they were able to unite the tribes and overcome the power of the magician Atotarho.

It is worth retracing how the Haudenosaunee paradigm shift took place. The Peacemaker, Deganawidah, was an exceptional individual who had grown up among the Hurons, north of Lake Ontario. Legends speak of his birth from a virgin and of many signs that accompanied it. From early on, Deganawidah knew that he had to perform his mission away from home and that it would be related to bringing peace. When he came to manhood, he crossed the lake on a white canoe made of stone and reached Iroquois territory, which was mired in constant strife. There was perpetual war between the five tribes of the Haudenosaunee, and it was accompanied by cannibalism and acts of magic intending to bring harm to one's enemies.

To everybody, the Peacemaker extended his message of righteousness, or desire to see justice prevail; of health, which is harmony between mind and body; and of the law, or that power to enforce the common will, which has the backing of the Great Spirit.

Deganawidah could not accomplish anything until he found another human being who would accept his message in mind, heart, and will. This human being was Hiawatha, who had been a cannibal and who met the Peacemaker at a time in which he had started to question his cannibalistic habits. Hiawatha embraced the message wholeheartedly, intuiting how much it was needed by all the tribes. But he lived among the Onondagas, and close to him ruled the tyrant of the land, a certain Atotarho (also called Thahodado), whom we are told had a head covered with snakes, a twisted mind, and seven crooks in his body. He was the magician who held the land under his spell.

Hiawatha called meetings to rally his tribe to the message of the prophet. He did have success, but each time, the magician caused one of his daughters to die and finally his wife as well. Broken in heart and in spirit, Hiawatha wandered the land, still committed to the prophet's message. He could not find solace, nor could anyone offer it to him. At length, over time, his pain lessened, and he realized that he could carry the sorrow of his people and bring consolation to others. This led him to devise the Ritual of Condolence, which includes the "Requickening Address." With it he knew he could bring consolation to all who were suffering.

The Peacemaker, in spirit, had been following closely the progress of his companion. He saw him perform the Ritual of Condolence and realized at that moment that Hiawatha was ready to receive the final healing. Deganawidah himself performed a Ritual of Condolence on Hiawatha. Now, we could say, teacher and pupil were equal. Both knew the depth of the message that wanted to shape the "New Mind."

Together, Deganawidah and Hiawatha summoned the tribes.

Whereas before they had been reluctant, now all could see that Hiawatha was like a new man. The tribes united and confronted the tyrant of the land, who tried all the magic he knew against them. He summoned the elements against them but saw that his strength no longer matched the new strength of the tribes who were acquiring the New Mind.

The tribes came into the presence of Atotarho. Hiawatha sang the song of peace and combed the snakes out of the magician's hair. The prophet healed him of his twisted mind and the crooks in his body. This event was central to the forming of the Haudenosaunee League, or the League of Five Nations. There was no need for revenge now that Atotarho had been healed. In fact, to him was given the highest ceremonial role, that of calling the tribes in council. The new confederacy did away with the rights of the single chief and established the tribes as equal in the affairs of governance. It is easy to remember the wise system of governance that the Iroquois established without honoring the events that led to its birth.

The Power of Two: Integration of Polarities

Deganawidah and Hiawatha worked to promote the redemption of Iroquois culture and could do so because they complemented each other in many ways. What one could not do, the other could; alone, neither could have achieved his goal. Without Hiawatha, Deganawidah's word would not have had a form. Without Deganawidah, Hiawatha would not have asked himself the most important questions regarding his people and himself. The message that the prophet spread among the Iroquois would not have been completed without someone willing to live it to its bitter end. That one was Hiawatha, who had to fully acquire the New Mind before his people could unite. The Message, the New Mind, and a new social form followed a sequence in the process leading to the forming of the confederacy. The Haudenosaunee League inaugurated centuries of peaceful coexistence between the tribes. It inspired the surrounding nations. And many colonists, Benjamin Franklin included, took renewed inspiration from its culture.

Like Deganawidah, Benjamin Franklin had intuited the future of America long before anyone else had started dreaming of it. He saw it as a possibility, as a departure from all forms of the past, as a hope for the future of humanity. He worked in both the New and the Old World to bring the new idea to birth. With the Declaration of Independence, the message started to take on a body, thanks to the contributions of Jefferson, Madison, Mason, and many others. But something else was needed, something crucial. The new idea had to find an individual ready to walk a completely new path, an individual who had the ability to do everything that had been done in the past (i.e., exert the full measure of his natural strength, assume power, and make himself a king) and who yet chose to do the contrary. The new social compact needed that lived example in order to create a break with the past. George Washington endured all the hesitations, temptations, delays, and weaknesses of his countrymen with the sole purpose of bringing to birth a reality that he intuited with his whole soul. He had to defeat all inner hesitation, all old habits and impulses that ran counter to the need of the time. Through his uprightness and determination, Washington rendered effective the vision that lived in Franklin's mind and spirit. Two completely different individuals harmonized their energy and united with many other remarkable souls to bring about another watershed moment in history.

Three or four centuries after the foundation of the Haudenosaunee League, the US Constitutional Convention also experienced a unique process of social integration. The long, harrowing hours of discussion given to ironing out issues were possible only because of the moral stature of many individuals present (chief among them, Washington and Franklin) and because the participants were open to hearing many perspectives, while being soberly realistic about what could be achieved.

The fate of the Bill of Rights was emblematic of all these developments. The first suggestion for the addition of such a document had been made by George Mason just five days before the end of the Philadelphia Convention. Later, the idea was reintroduced by James Madison, a Federalist, in order to appease the Anti-Federalists. Madison wanted to avoid a second Constitutional Convention, which might have undone all the difficult compromises of the first, and he hoped that the amendments would increase the government's popular support. The bill was influenced by earlier documents such as the English Bill of Rights, but most of all by the Virginia Declaration of Rights, which George Mason had written in 1776. Many of the amendments Madison proposed came from the drafting done by the Anti-Federalist George Mason. Madison proposed twenty amendments, and the House narrowed these to seventeen. The Senate edited them further and condensed them to twelve. In the process of ratification by the states, ten of the twelve survived.

On a continuum of possibilities presented to the states, one end of the spectrum would have meant violent revolution, and the other, dissolution. The American Revolution had most easily avoided the ideological extremes that had marred the French Revolution. It was far more difficult to counter centrifugal forces that could have kept the states aloof from a common effort. Either extreme would have made creation of a social compact and a nation impossible. The matter of slavery required a true element of creative compromise; without it, we could be almost certain that no new nation would have been born. Slavery itself formed a tremendous stumbling block, one that had no equivalent in the Iroquois compact. The unresolved issue came later to haunt the new nation.

The emancipation of the slaves during the Civil War and the campaign for civil rights in the 1950s and 1960s were steps in attempts to end the damage done by slavery and segregation. Women's suffrage was another important step in extending the meaning of political equality.

At the distance of three to four centuries, North American soil witnessed two cultural changes. Certainly, the American Revolution was incomplete—it did not resolve the problem of slavery; it only pointed to the possibility of extinguishing it. Though dramatically different in terms of cultures and dynamics, the two historical turning points had something in common. Both carried their main inspiration through key individuals who were strikingly different, but who also formed vital complements to each other. Both were the result of new worldviews. Constructive dialogue was the cornerstone of both cultural shifts.

The New American Experiential Spirituality: The Birth of Alcoholics Anonymous

Although the American Dream is now very diluted, hope comes from other quarters; its roots are growing under the surface and preparing future foundations for what will emerge above ground. A slow revolution of values has been made possible since the 1930s and 1940s; it continues to the present.

We saw in the previous chapter that Bill Wilson could effectively counter alcoholism only when he recognized the need to turn to a higher power for help. This, however, was only the first step. It was the key encounter with Bob Smith that added the other pillar of Alcoholics Anonymous: the need for human beings to help each other on the way to recovery. The horizontal collaboration with one's peers was as important as the vertical connection to a higher power.

Robert Smith was born in 1879, in St. Johnsbury, Vermont, about a hundred miles from Wilson's hometown. Smith presented a perfect complement to Wilson in temperament and upbringing. Wilson, the extrovert, basked in the limelight and tended to take center stage. Smith, the introvert, dreaded public exposure as much as he liked personal contact. Wilson, the restless innovator, was willing to try anything new; the more conservative Smith kept AA on solid ground.

The contrast between the two men is quite striking in the way each man distanced himself from alcohol. Wilson's awakening was an extraordinary experience, one given to few. It inevitably led him to feel special. Smith's unique contribution was the idea of making amends and restitution to all friends and acquaintances he had wronged. This step of tremendous will and courage is another keystone of AA. Smith did not lose his craving for alcohol all at once; he took what AA calls a path of vigorous action. Spiritual awakening and protracted human effort are the two goals for which AA struggles. Wilson was closer to the first; Smith to the second.

AA gave America hope where none had been found previously. And it did so in the most unexpected way. Doctors had all but given up on alcohol. Who could have predicted that alcoholics would be able to help fellow sufferers? And that AA could do so at no cost for the alcoholics, or individuals suffering all other kinds of addiction? The ideal of American equality triumphed against all odds. AA's anonymity is the ultimate emblem of healing done among peers.

The twelve-step program is but the best-known example of group work that affects our social reality. Also in this category are support groups and crisis hotlines for all kinds of individual and social ills, nonviolent communication, and the extensive landscape of social technology. We turn next to the last two of these.

Bridges over the Divides: Nonviolent Communication

Nonviolent communication (NVC), also called compassionate communication, stands somewhere between the twelve-step programs and social technology.[1] Whereas a twelve-step program addresses individual needs, and social technology serves organizational needs, NVC serves the purpose of communication between two individuals or groups.

NVC was developed by Marshall Rosenberg in the 1960s. It is primarily geared toward interpersonal communication, although it also works as a tool for personal development. NVC focuses on three aspects of communication: (1) self-expression—expressing oneself authentically in a way that is likely to be positively received by others; (2) empathy—listening with compassion; and (3) self-empathy—compassionate awareness of one's own feelings and needs (see Figure 3.1).

At the first level of an interaction or dialogue lies the need for accurate observation. What is it that defines observation and distinguishes it from interpretation? Our familiar language lays many traps. We often say things such as "You are *always* late" or "You *never* do ..." when we may say more correctly, "Four times out of the last five, you were late" or "You haven't done the jobs you promised me, twice already." Language that is not truly reflective of reality is, by definition, alienating.

At another level is everything we try to define in the emotional realm. Here, too, we can remain objective (e.g., "I feel/am upset, hurt, sad, angry") or exit into the realm of interpretation (e.g., "I feel manipulated, rejected, abandoned"), of which nothing can be said with certainty. When I say words like *manipulated* or *abandoned*, I immediately project an interpretation of somebody's intention into my feelings, by implying that the other person had the intention to manipulate or abandon me. At this level, a key distinction needs to be expressed. In the realm of feelings and their expression, we often confuse stimulus and cause. The stimulus that meets us externally triggers an inner reaction, which is what we are calling "cause." No two individuals react in the same way to external stimuli, whether a source of joy or pain or anything in between. An expression such as "You *make* me angry" blurs the distinction between cause and stimulus and detracts from the ability to take responsibility for our feelings. Going a step further, feelings that are not pertinently expressed and/or inwardly apprehended form a barrier to one's understanding of needs and to self-connection.

Moving deeper into knowing ourselves, we arrive at the expression of our needs. Here, too, language can reflect that we are truly in touch with our objective needs and aware of them—as in "I need respect, assistance, support, communication, growth, self-expression, freedom." Or our language may reflect that we are alienated from our deeper self— as in "I need you to be nicer to me; I need you to do what I want; I need a new car, career, girl/boyfriend, in order to be happy." In the first example, we are expressing what individuals want and need in a universal way; in the second, the needs of the individual concern external factors instead of the self. When we express a need in a universal manner, we are not depriving anybody else of his or her freedom. Needs, when truly understood and expressed in a universal way, are not mutually exclusive. My desire for comfort, safety, or respect need never be expressed at the expense of anyone else's comfort, safety, or respect. My desire for someone to be nicer to me imposes upon the other person my expectations of what "being nice" means. A need expressed in those terms is neither universal nor conducive to productive communication and connection.

Once we master the three aforementioned steps, we are ready to express true requests rather than demands. A demand has only one response possible. Formulating a true request is tied to the ability to imagine a great variety of outcomes that satisfy the needs of two parties in a conversation.

NVC assumes that all human beings have the capacity for compassion and that they resort to violence (whether overt or covert) only when they do not have access to effective strategies for meeting needs, other than those they receive from the dominant culture. Nonviolent communication works from the realization and experience that all human behavior is a means to meet universal human needs. When we can think in terms of needs, rather than the strategies to meet

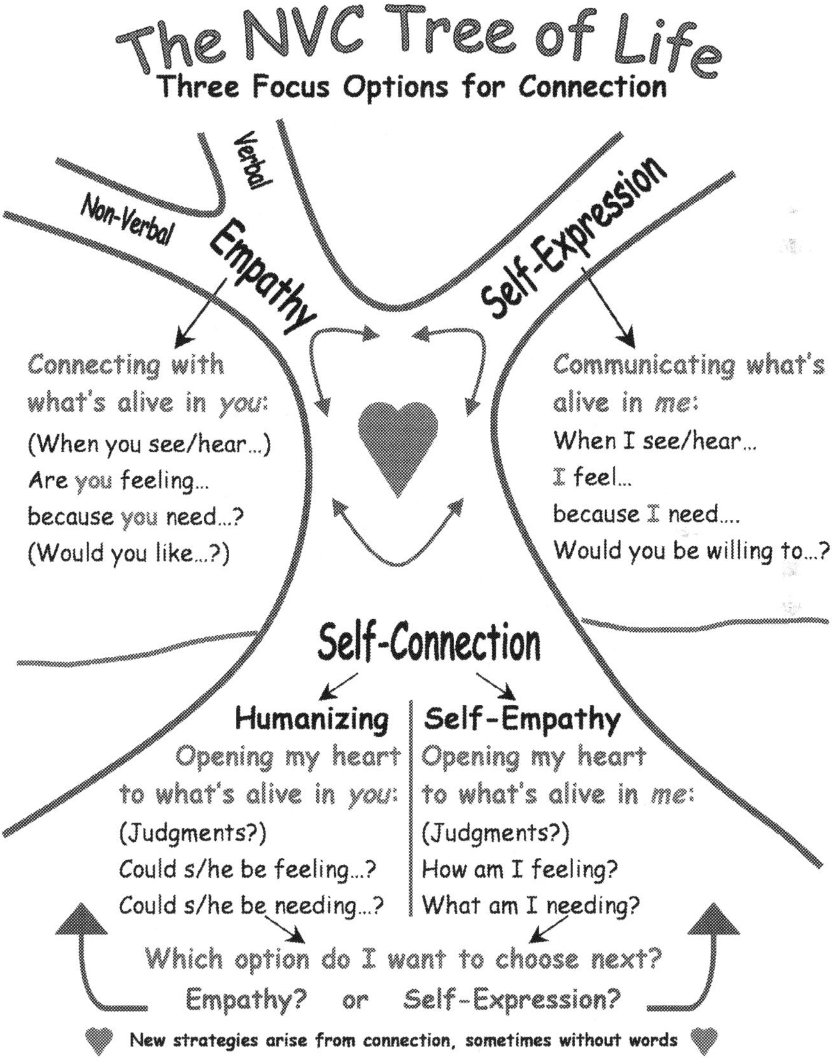

The NVC Tree of Life
Three Focus Options for Connection

Non-Verbal

Verbal

Empathy

Self-Expression

Connecting with
what's alive in *you*:
(When you see/hear...)
Are *you* feeling...
because *you* need...?
(Would you like...?)

Communicating what's
alive in *me*:
When I see/hear...
I feel...
because I need....
Would you be willing to...?

Self-Connection

Humanizing	**Self-Empathy**
Opening my heart to what's alive in *you*: (Judgments?) Could s/he be feeling...? Could s/he be needing...?	Opening my heart to what's alive in *me*: (Judgments?) How am I feeling? What am I needing?

Which option do I want to choose next?
Empathy?   or   Self-Expression?

New strategies arise from connection, sometimes without words

Figure 3.1: The NVC Tree of Life (Inbal Kashtan, www.cnvc.org, www.baynvc.org).

those needs, we can effectively eschew conflict. This requires willingness to slow down the conversation and go to the root of the issue (the needs), rather than stay on its surface (strategies). In effect, if we can identify our own needs, the needs of others, and the feelings that surround these needs, harmony can be achieved.

An NVC mediation illustrates most clearly the process of nonviolent communication. Such mediation is a process in which a facilitator helps the participants in forming a true connection at the level of feelings and needs before coming to common resolutions. A true mediation can occur only after the participants experience a qualitative shift in themselves and in their relationship. Typically, when the two parties feel heard with the help of the mediator, they offer clear signs of relaxation and openness. This is not a place of compromise, but a true shift to the higher level of meeting the needs of both parties.

NVC is much more than a technique of communication. It is a paradigm shift for stepping into a new reality that honors the deepest aspirations of two parties. It completely eschews the notion of compromise in favor of mutual satisfaction, the stepping-stone for consensus. These ideas can be taken further in working at larger dimensions of social reality. We will now explore social technology, from one of the expressions of its beginnings to the extensive set of applications that are possible today.

The Early Days of Social Technology: The Institute of Cultural Affairs

In 1954 the World Council of Churches met in Evanston, Illinois, and decided to create a center for the training of laypersons in North America. Christian businessmen in Chicago founded the Evanston Institute of Ecumenical Studies.[2]

At the same time a group of Christian students and staff of the University of Texas, calling themselves the Christian Faith and Life Community, started to research the relationship between faith and contemporary life. Under the direction of Dr. Joseph W. Matthews, the group designed a curriculum for students and laity. It acquired the name of Religious Studies I.

In 1962 the Evanston Institute, now called the Ecumenical Institute, appointed Dr. Matthews as its new dean. Moving to Chicago, he brought with him the seven families from Texas who had been focused on a comprehensive life of Christian worship, study, and service. At this time the Order: Ecumenical was begun, formed primarily by families of volunteers. It was modeled after known religious family orders, and the seven families played a central role at its inception.

The mission of the order was church renewal and community development. The groups followed three directions with consistency: education, research, and implementation. The pioneering curriculum emphasized whole-system models. A bold and successful experiment of comprehensive community development was its first step of implementation. It was called Fifth City, a comprehensive experiment in urban renewal, of which more will be said in chapter 4. What started as an ecumenical initiative soon turned into much more than an effort to work between denominations and renew faith. In acknowledgment of this reality, in 1973 the organization renamed itself the Institute for Cultural Affairs (ICA), by which it is still known at present.

From the curriculum evolved two interrelated outcomes. The seminal experiment of Fifth City continued, with development projects all over the world. The social process of change was nurtured by tools such as the focused conversation, consensus workshop, action planning, participatory strategic planning, and so on. The tools here mentioned form part of a whole known as "technology of participation" within ICA. These are processes through which an organization can move away from majority rule toward consensus. Through its technology of participation ICA has achieved the very goal of systems-thinking—to bring to life a whole that is larger than the sum of its parts. Central to ICA's idea of social development was the idea that new outcomes would be possible when all stakeholders in a given issue could feel heard and experience that they were equal partners in the search for a solution. From the premises of greater openness to its environment and fuller participation of all its individuals, any given organization can find within itself the resources that can help it respond to internal and/ or external challenges and generate lasting change. Next we will look at the simplest of such processes: the focused conversation.[3]

The focused conversation is used for many goals: addressing a topic of study, setting an informal conversation for social purpose, reviewing an event, and exploring different perspectives. Such a conversation allows participants to raise issues, expand perspectives, quickly gather data from a large group, get to the heart of the matter, and see a whole picture.

The focused conversation involves a dialogue at four successive levels:

- Objective level (perception): questions about facts and external reality
- Reflective level (response): internal response to the data; feelings, moods, emotions, memories, images, and associations of ideas
- Interpretive level (judgment): questions to draw out meaning, values, significance, and implications
- Decisional level (decision): step to elicit resolution, bring the conversation to a close, and make resolves about the future

Our usual conversation moves back and forth between the aforementioned levels and often omits most of the uncomfortable reflective level. It is not unusual to believe that strong feelings and emotions can only wreck a meeting, and for good cause. However, the charge present in an emotion will resurface in the interpretive and decision-making levels. The focused conversation gives personal reactions their due by raising them earlier in the conversation and confining their effect over the rest of the dialogue. Acknowledged feelings, bias, prejudice, and gut reactions make the subsequent levels of the conversation easier to address because everybody knows what stands behind concerns and criticisms that will be raised. When the previous levels have been addressed exhaustively, the group will reach a conclusion and a decision, if needed, in a way that will feel very natural. Everybody will come out with a feeling of contentment, a feeling of having been heard and having contributed.

The reader may recognize that the focused conversation carries forward what was said about nonviolent communication. The objective level corresponds to the observation of NVC; the reflective level to the feelings; the interpretive to the needs; and the decision-making to the requests. All of this is quite simply close to universal phenomena, and we will see more of it as we look at Theory U.

Technology of Participation—with all its facilitation processes over and above the focused conversation—makes possible decision making through enhanced participation. It has tackled complex organizational and community issues by integrating the needs of all stakeholders, be they employees, members of a community, management, shareholders, external parties affected by an organization's policies or actions, or local NGOs. In a successful process the whole resonates through the integration of all the parts—internal and external stakeholders—and everyone plays a part as an equal. When the process is honored, everyone has the definite feeling of having been heard and having contributed, a feeling that the entire group is stepping together into a collective reality that is fulfilling a common calling.

After the spread of Technology of Participation and of the Quaker-derived consensus decision making, many other approaches found their way into organizational change. Some examples are Appreciative Inquiry, Study Circles, and Bohmian Dialogue. In the last two decades this work has expanded almost exponentially, and there are simply too many approaches to list them all here. Among those about which the public may hear most often are World Café (see Sidebar 3.1), Conversation Cafés, Open Space Technology, Future Search, and dialogue and deliberation.

Networks and Innovations: Developments in Social Technology

In the last ten to twenty years, social technology has entered an exponential phase of development. The second edition of *The Change Handbook* (2007) lists sixty-one social technology approaches presently available.[4] Its previous edition, published eight years earlier, counted only eighteen processes. And many are still not listed; Theory U, which we will discuss next, is a point in case.

SIDEBAR 3.1: World Café Guidelines and Model

(Reprinted with kind permission of Avril Orloff and
the World Café, http://www.theworldcafe.com/.)

The World Café methodology is a simple, effective, and flexible format for hosting large group dialogue. The basic model comprises the following five components, quoted from the World Café website (http://www.theworldcafe.com/method.html).

1) Setting: Create a "special" environment, most often modeled after a café, i.e. small round tables covered with a checkered tablecloth, butcher block paper, colored pens, a vase of flowers, and optional "talking stick" item. There should be four chairs at each table.

2) Welcome and Introduction: The host begins with a warm welcome and an introduction to the World Café process, setting the context, sharing the Cafe Etiquette, and putting participants at ease.

3) Small Group Rounds: The process begins with the first of three or more twenty minute rounds of conversation for the small group seated around a table. At the end of the twenty minutes, each member of the group moves to a different new table. They may or may not choose to leave one person as the "table host" for the next round, who welcomes the next group and briefly fills them in on what happened in the previous round.

4) Questions: each round is prefaced with a question designed for the specific context and desired purpose of the session. The same questions can be used for more than one round, or they can be built upon each other to focus the conversation or guide its direction.

5) Harvest: After the small groups (and/or in between rounds, as desired) individuals are invited to share insights or other results from their conversations with the rest of the large group. These results are reflected visually in a variety of ways, most often using graphic recorders in the front of the room.

Facilitators often mix and blend approaches. An event may start with a World Café, continue with an Open Space, and end with a Future Search conference, to offer just one example. And the use of social technology has extended from the organizational level to addressing the goals of extended networks of organizations coming from all sectors of society.

Otto Scharmer's Theory U has offered an overarching understanding of the principles at work not only in social technology but also in the twelve steps, nonviolent communication, and the entire set of experiential tools of transformation that now constellate American culture.[5] Basically, Otto Scharmer saw that in the process of collective transformation and emergence, we must pass through three successive steps: the transformation of the way we think, the way we feel, and the way we act. Scharmer has called these stages open mind, open heart, and open will. When the three have been achieved, we collectively step into a new reality in which new, unforeseen possibilities emerge that meet the agreement of all stakeholders and that free tremendous energy for implementation.

Let us examine the situation of an organization (a public agency, a business, a corporation, a nonprofit organization, or a network), and let us consider as its stakeholders not only those who work within the organization but also all those who have a stake in its work. Stakeholders for a corporation that imports third-world food products are not only the corporation's employees, management, and suppliers but also its consumers, the third-world producers, the NGOs that work in those countries in relation to food production, environmental organizations, and so forth.

When all the significant stakeholders in a situation are called to express their views in a conversational format that encourages true dialogue, people can finally start to see the tapestry of elements that contribute to form a situation of conflict and dissonance, or of harmony and progress. Clarity is reached about the complexity of factors that contribute to a given group dynamic. This is the stage of the open mind in which all contributions are welcome, and debate is channeled toward positive outcomes.

From the first level of the open mind, the participants can start to see patterns emerging and realize that they have unconsciously been part of the patterns. Reality will appear in all its complexity, showing participants the one-sidedness of their previous judgments. This stage may be overwhelming, but it is a precondition for loosening previous perceptions and allowing the new to form.

Individuals and groups are later encouraged to take responsibility for their part in the collective patterns. Each stakeholder group can understand with empathy the perspectives of the other stakeholder groups. This is what encourages connection between stakeholders at the level of feelings and what Scharmer calls the work of the open heart.

Only after this stage has been experienced can visions and options for action emerge. When the process is completed, a shift takes place that allows the participants to acknowledge a common ground from which they can operate, allied with a new enthusiasm and desire for moving into concerted action through the open will. Going through this stage means being able to let go of predetermined solutions or favored outcomes.

The open will sets the stage for something new that can finally emerge through presencing (from presence and sensing). All individuals have now reached a willingness to let go of everything that ties them to the past and to trust the process and the wisdom that is present in the whole. Presencing is a space in which the past is put on hold, and the participants can collectively listen to the future that wants to emerge. Letting go makes room for a process of allowing or, in Scharmer's words, "letting come."

Presencing is an all-encompassing experience; any single individual can apprehend only some facets of it. Following are examples of individual perceptions. "When I am part of a social field that crosses the threshold at the bottom of the U, it feels as if I am participating in the birth of a new world. It is a profound, quieting experience; I feel as if I've been touched by eternal beauty. There is a deep opening of my higher Self," offers Betty Sue Flowers. For Joseph Jaworski, "moving through the bottom of the U is becoming aware of the incredible beauty of life itself, of becoming re-enchanted with the world ... When the sort of commitment you are talking about happens, you feel as if you're fulfilling your destiny, but you also feel as if you're freer than you've ever been in your life. It's a huge paradox." Otto Scharmer echoes them: "For me, the core of Presencing is waking up together—waking up to who we really are by linking with and acting from our highest future Self—and by using the Self as a vehicle for bringing forth new worlds."[6] In these words we can sense how deeply spiritual a process can be that does not originate from a religious or spiritual doctrine, or from a desire for spiritual experience.

After presencing, the group moves into the implementation of the process. At the stage of crystallizing, what emerges as an insight, a simple place of openness, almost a place of vacuum in the idea of presencing, needs to acquire focus and direction. Ideas need to be built upon and solidified, and key players need to find each other and determine what forms their initiatives should take.

At the next stage, *Theory U* introduces the idea of prototyping, which means nurturing and sustaining pilot initiatives for testing concrete ideas on a small scale and offering all of these the needed support in order to later integrate the practices on larger scales. When pilot initiatives are successful, change is then brought to the level of the entire organization.

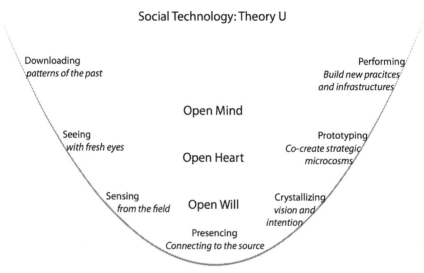

Figure 3.2: Theory U: going through the open mind, open heart, and open will (modified from Scharmer, *Theory U: Leading from the Emerging Future*).

When this holistic way of working is integrated at each step of the way in the organization, we can talk about performing. This word means more than integrating the new; it extends to ensuring that the processes described earlier are sustained on an ongoing basis, that they become the internal culture of the organization. For that purpose, the organization must set in place structures and processes that allow it to operate in a new way.

The diagram of the U is what links together seemingly heterogeneous levels of experience: twelve-step, nonviolent communication, and social technology. Let's trace briefly how. Theory U adds the clarity of the central step of all these approaches, which is generally neglected, since it is the most subtle: presencing.

In Alcoholics Anonymous, steps 1 to 3 ask the recovering addict to turn to the higher power, the stage that corresponds to the open mind. Steps 4 to 7 ask a further effort culminating in the compilation of a moral inventory—a list of everything that weighs on the soul. Healing can proceed only if the alcoholic allows herself to feel everything that the drug suppressed by opening the heart. Going through steps 8 and 9, which require us to make amends for everything we did under the influence of alcohol, means facing powerlessness and the possibility of self-forgiveness. This is the stage of the open will, which culminates in presencing, when the individual acquires a sense of the working of the higher power.

Briefly, the stages that follow are continuing to take personal inventory (step 10), equivalent to crystallizing; turning to prayer and meditation (step 11), the equivalent of prototyping; and taking the message to others (step 12), equivalent to spreading the culture of twelve-step, which corresponds to performing.

The examples of nonviolent communication and focused conversation include only four steps. The first three correspond to the left side of the U. The fourth is not mentioned but is what makes communication and group conversations effective. The last step is a mix of crystallizing and prototyping. Step 7 (performing) appears only with repeated practice.

The step of the open mind corresponds to observation in NVC; open heart corresponds to feelings; and open will corresponds to needs. When a communication is successful at these levels, an opening occurs, which is experienced in mutual openness and ability to relax and trust (presencing). The participants can then experiment with making requests (crystallizing) and determine which requests they will test in the future (prototyping).

The focused conversation begins with the objective level, an obvious manifestation of the open mind. The open heart is found in the willingness to face the discomfort of the inner reaction in the reflective level. The open will is faced in the interpretive level, in which participants collectively find meaning and create the openness (presencing) for something new to take place. When everybody reaches a new place, action steps can be offered (crystallizing), and among these, some are selected and others rejected (prototyping).

Let us return now to social technology. It is not only the clarity reached in social technology that characterizes the 1990s and the turn of the twentieth century, but also the application of social technology to larger and larger networks, rather than just single organizations. Witness the Global Compact that brought together worldwide leaders from the private and public sectors, unions, and NGOs, in the promotion of socially responsible businesses worldwide.[7]

Sustainable Food Lab is another initiative incorporating more than one hundred businesses, government organizations, and NGOs worldwide, trying prototypes of alternative and sustainable food systems.[8] Sustainable Food Lab integrates Theory U with approaches from the Society for Organizational Learning. This expanding work of facilitation and integration is now a powerful tool for the emergence of tri-sector partnerships—the working together of public, private, and nonprofit sectors.

Social technology is only the natural continuation and improvement of the processes of deliberation that saw their birth in North America with the Haudenosaunee Confederacy, the American Revolution, the Constitutional Convention, and the adoption of the Bill of Rights. In the last two proceedings, a tremendous amount of effort and energy went toward creative compromise. These were compromises that would accommodate large and small states; a strong central government and true federalism; and the different economies of the North and South. This was more than abdication to mere necessity; it was the result of the art of listening with open mind, heart, and will. However, fateful compromise also crept into the Constitution, chiefly in the agreements on slavery.

What originated with the Haudenosaunee, the Constitution, and the Bill of Rights has now been revived and metamorphosed in social technology. What we are to contemplate next offers a whole new meaning to governance of and by the people.

New Democracy: Reclaiming "We the People"

The question naturally arises, would it be possible to extend these participatory approaches to governance itself? And how difficult would this change be? To anticipate, let us simply indicate that not only is such a change possible, but also the art and science of this momentous shift (a great part of which has seen its birth in this country) has already been established and has gained ground over the last forty years. It has also been tested and has offered remarkably positive results.

Representative democracy as it is presently practiced more often than not gathers the fruit of common foolishness, rather than collective intelligence and wisdom. The power of money and corporate interests in the system completely clouds the reality of the issues and controls the way information is spread. We could place our hope in more direct forms of democracy. But neither does this offer a solution, because it often depends on who is there and what groups have the greatest vested interests and/or the power to mobilize people, not necessarily on the wisdom of the whole. Involving millions of people in deliberation actually reduces the likelihood of wise outcomes because of difficulties in facilitating the process, offering equal access to information, gathering the results, and so forth. Much of direct democracy lacks full inquiry and facilitated deliberation, so that it rarely taps into public wisdom— rather, the contrary.

Notwithstanding these limitations, there is now a way to strengthen participatory democracy by availing ourselves of the insights generated by social technology. This means, first of all, changing the kind of polarized conversations we have at present to ones that meet the following criteria:

- Participants can distinguish facts from lies, distortions, and manipulations of the truth. Participants can see the entire complexity of the situation and still come up with creative outcomes because information comes from a variety of sources and is made more easily accessible and understandable.
- Everyone present feels heard (and those absent feel their voices are represented).

- Participants are clearly told how the conversation will be conducted and how the results will be used; there is complete transparency.
- Participants will be safe no matter what differences, disturbances, and emotions emerge in the process.

In our present ideas of democracy, we hear only the voices of the parts, and for a certain amount of time, one part prevails over the other; then the roles reverse. We can safely say that never are the needs of the whole met. This is the ultimate reality built into the two-party system; it is a preprogrammed premise for failure, one that excludes reaching common ground.

In contrast to this well-known system, experiences worldwide have shown that it is possible to engage the full spectrum of the population through a small number of citizens who form a microcosm of We the People, with the full diversity of relevant information, in ways that help them find authentic common ground. Dialogue and deliberation in the form of citizen deliberative councils (of which more will be said shortly) is an approach that brings to expression the reality of We the People in the sense of Lincoln's "government of the people, by the people, for the people."

The intelligence of We the People is not directly related to the intelligence of the individual members present in the decision-making process. We know the opposite quite well. Very intelligent and competent people can generate a phenomenal amount of collective foolishness, along with detrimental short-term planning and implementation, simply by getting in each other's way or by lacking relevant information and perspectives in their analysis. In contrast, through dialogue and deliberation techniques, it is possible for the voice of We the People to emerge as a reality. There are a great variety of deliberative methods for channeling differences and conflicts toward new insight and positive co-creative outcomes.

New possibilities have emerged through convening a small group of very diverse citizens—that is, a cross section of all stakeholder groups, selected in a statistically significant random fashion—and holding conversations and deliberations through tested methods of facilitation.

Such so-called citizen deliberative councils (CDCs) have been held all over the United States and the world over the last forty years. And they have had remarkable success. The councils are temporary and serve only for the specific issue they are called to consider; they speak with a voice that transcends right-left political divides and accurately represents the community.[9]

Citizen Deliberative Councils and Their Formats

The members of citizen deliberative councils (CDCs) consider how best to address an issue after receiving ample and thorough information from a wide variety of sources and after harmonizing a whole spectrum of diverse, and often contrasting, perspectives. The following are eight characteristics of a CDC[10]:

- It is a face-to-face assembly.
- It comprises from twelve to two hundred citizens selected randomly and demographically, in order to reflect the wide variety of stakeholders and all possible perspectives present in the community that the process addresses. Groups should be neither too large (expensive and time-consuming) nor too small (not statistically significant).
- It convenes for a set time (a few days to a few weeks).
- CDC members act as peers; roles and titles are set aside for the time of the deliberations.
- It requires skillful facilitation to allow all perspectives to be aired and heard.
- The group has a specific mandate that allows it to address a situation, concern, issue, proposal, budget, or similar issue.
- Accurate information, in the form of inclusive, balanced briefing materials, interviews, and presentations by experts and advocates, is provided to the council.
- The process reaches completion when the council drafts a report that details the findings and recommendations to the authority that convened the CDC, the electorate, the concerned community, the media, and so forth.

The new often has surprising deep roots into the past. This system of randomly forming the CDCs has an important and little-appreciated precedent in the democracy of ancient Athens. From the fifth century BC, Athenians drew lots to select 90 percent of their political representatives (five hundred members chosen by lot among the population above age thirty). Elections were used only for choosing top generals and assigning financial positions. Athenians considered their random choice central to their democracy.

Citizen deliberative councils have been used with a variety of evolving formats. Two formats that have developed in the United States and have been most used here are citizen juries and wisdom councils. Citizen juries, designed by political scientist Ned Crosby, may be one of the most widely used models worldwide. These involve twelve to twenty-four citizens selected by random stratified sampling who interview experts and deliberate during a period of three to five days. The Minneapolis-based Jefferson Center, a nonpartisan, nonprofit organization dedicated to strengthening democracy, convened thirty-two citizen juries in the period from 1974 to 2012 in the United States. The model has been introduced in the United Kingdom by the Institute for Public Policy Research and is widely used there.

Wisdom councils were conceived in 1993 by Jim Rough, who had already developed his "dynamic facilitation," a process designed to strengthen group members' participation and unleash their emergent creativity. The councils further evolved into the creative insight councils (CICs), which gather from one to two dozen randomly selected citizens to explore an issue or a proposal through dynamic facilitation. The process is ultimately designed to stimulate creative thinking to address a situation or issue, not necessarily to form detailed proposals. A CIC appeals to experts for information input, and the results can be given back to experts to generate more inclusive proposals, which would then go back to the CIC. Wisdom Councils and CICs have been held in North America and in Austria.

Citizen deliberative councils can serve multiple functions, such as

- providing periodic citizen-based state of the union declarations;
- studying issues on behalf of public officials, in order to provide voters with balanced information and guidance on issues, based on the community's core values (as these are reflected in the diversity of the selected citizens);
- reviewing proposed ballot initiatives and referenda, reducing special interest manipulations in the framing of the issues;
- proposing ballot initiatives to deal with identified issues;
- ensuring a sober public evaluation of controversial legislation;
- reviewing candidates for elected public office, wherein one or more CDCs could evaluate candidates for each of the issues targeted (economy, environment, security, and so forth), evaluate their qualifications, or assess candidates' personalities;
- reviewing government budgets, which has proved to generate support for taxes after the citizens realize the importance of the needs they want to address; and
- reviewing government or corporate performance.

Public wisdom quite definitely will change the dynamic of power in many ways. Whether they would receive a sphere of power of their own or serve in an advisory capacity, wisdom councils and CICs would

- enable We the People to have direct say and power over important issues society faces;
- advise our leaders through a voice that is respected by a vast majority of the population regardless of political, religious, or philosophical convictions;
- represent the core values of the community by embracing its diverse perspectives, needs, and aspirations;
- call public officials to accountability;
- inform the citizens by considering all possible scenarios, both positive and negative, in the short, medium, and long term;
- stimulate the general public to take action on issues of common interest; and
- use expert knowledge in a concerted way and confine experts to the role of advisers.

Citizen deliberative councils have offered inspiring results in supporting and strengthening direct democracy, the most ordinary forms of which are the referendum and the citizen ballot initiative process. The way in which these are named, framed, publicized, and advertised offers many entry points to special interests.

In 2011 Oregon's official Citizen's Initiative Review established the CDC process by law to review ballot initiatives and referenda on behalf of the voters. The process is transparent, and the results are offered in the official voter information pamphlets; it uses the citizen jury methodology, with eighteen to twenty-four randomly selected registered voters convened for five days to hear from advocates on any side of the issue and offer their conclusions to the voters. The so-called citizen statement, printed in the official voter pamphlets, offers a balance between the opposite partisan promotions of the issues. John Gastil and Katie Knobolch investigated at length the results of these initiatives. The voters who read the statements appreciated becoming more knowledgeable about the measures; and in the instance of Oregon's 2010 measures 73 (minimum criminal sentence increase) and 74 (legalizing the sale of medical marijuana), those voters were much less likely to support the measures.[11]

Presently, the interest in citizen initiative reviews is spreading to California, Idaho, and Colorado. If so used, these CDCs will offer correctives to poorly designed initiatives, or measures that are slanted toward special interests and designed to manipulate the electorate. Ideally, proposed legislation could receive the input of a CDC convened for the specific purpose, receive new formulation by lawmakers or those who help them in the task, and then be returned to a new CDC for improving the quality of the initiatives, their usefulness to the community, and their likelihood to be approved by large majorities.

A more comprehensive example of the usefulness of CDCs in the process of sociopolitical deliberations was demonstrated by the groundbreaking initiative promoted by Canadian magazine *Maclean's* in June 1991, a time in which the country suffered a crisis of identity and the very serious threat of secession by Quebec. A team of three American facilitators, with Roger Fisher as the leader, led twelve participants, representing all the major sectors of public opinion and demographics in Canada, to come up with a common vision for the future of their country, under the title People's Verdict. This simpler process succeeded where a parliamentary committee, a $27 million Citizen's Forum on Canada's Future, and a government consultation initiative involving four hundred thousand Canadians had previously failed.[12]

Through the citizen deliberative councils, far more than the sum of the parts emerges, much like what we have seen in social technology. "People 'lose themselves' in the group, not by becoming smaller or less themselves, but by expanding to embrace more of the group's interactive power within their own capacities and responses," Tom Atlee says in describing the experience of countless participants. And he restates this dimension of practical spirituality: "Whatever connects us to our core commons, the heart and the soul of our connection to each other and the world, is spiritual to me. And high quality conversation draws us into the connection in a very clean and simple way, with no need for any spiritual language or sectarian or esoteric beliefs or practices."[13]

The practical examples of public deliberation offered so far are an avenue to discovering our shared humanity and aliveness, beyond political, cultural, religious, and ideological mind-sets. Allowing the voice of the whole to determine the common good moves us from political thinking (the 51 percent majority) to finding common ground in supermajorities (67 percent or more), or even near-consensus. A narrow majority will not be wise; oftentimes it will consider only the short term, and the results it determines will not be long-lasting. Wider cultural agreement taps into the power and knowledge that lives at the edge of the system (all the information available) rather than what can be provided by experts or politicians.

Citizen Legislatures as a Fourth Branch of Government

The long-cherished dream of equality can be expanded even further. Ethan J. Leib (*Deliberative Democracy in America: A Proposal for a Popular Branch of Government*), Ernest Callenbach (*A Citizen Legislature*), Tom Atlee (*Empowering Public Wisdom: A Practical Vision of Citizen-Led Politics*), and others are envisioning how our system of government could be modified, with the smallest effort, to actively include We the People in its deliberations and legislation.[14] Citizen legislatures, as a new branch of government, could be implemented at all levels: federal, state, and local governments. They would be an empowered legislative body made up of randomly selected citizens.

Once in session, the citizen legislature (CL) would publicize its findings and become known and appreciated for its service to the population. Atlee considers that such an assembly should number 450 people at the federal level, in order to represent the country's diversity. The statistical margin of error at 400 is about 5 percent; it lowers to only 3 percent at 1,100, but the costs rise considerably. (The margin of error is determined by comparing how a representative group of people stands in relation to an issue when compared to a much larger sample or the whole population.) In order to account for the small margin of error, the new political body would be required to operate at a supermajority vote of 67 percent, or even 75 to 80 percent for major issues. The supermajority requirement is a powerful incentive for crafting higher-quality legislation that satisfies the needs of most constituencies.

Pay for service in the legislature could be set at levels comparable to that of presently elected officials to induce people to accept the assignment and involve themselves in the task seriously. Service in this chosen body would be equivalent to that of jury duty. With the plenary body rotated in shifts of thirds, the new hires would have an apprenticeship period under the wing of the more seasoned members. Naturally, the process should be assisted by a top-notch facilitation staff.

In the long run, the CL could even replace the congressional House of Representatives, to balance out state interests with those of a body that represents the whole without claiming privileges for their states or districts in a partisan way. The citizen deliberative council panels formed from within the CL could simply counsel Congress and the president, or they could also introduce new legislation. The CL could conduct various deliberations simultaneously; it could even hold simultaneous CDCs on the same issues or bills (i.e., using three CDCs of seventy members each) and compare the results. If these agreed with each other, legislation could be drafted from their conclusions.

If a bill received a supermajority assent (67 percent or more) in the CL, it could then be sent to the Senate. The Senate could override the bill with another supermajority. The reverse could occur at the same time: the Senate could draft legislation to be sent to the CL, which could override it with a supermajority vote. This collaboration would heighten the quality of legislation and induce greater collaboration between representative bodies. Nothing else would be changed in relation to the powers of the executive or the judicial branches of the federal government.

From Democratic to Participatory: True Equality beyond the Party System

Citizen deliberative councils, and social technologies in general, promise a methodology for stepping into possible futures that respect the needs of all stakeholders involved. This is a step away from the old democracy, or the will of the majority, toward participatory decision making with consensus from all parties (supermajorities in the case of CDCs).

Consensus here means a great level of assent, not necessarily unanimity. For some, consensus may mean complete satisfaction; for others it would be something they can accept and hope to improve. For all, consensus represents common ground and the evolving awareness that none of us can have satisfaction at the expense of someone else or live in a continuous tug-of-war, in which part of society is always waiting for its turn to subvert what the previous part has established.

The present political system in the United States has been undermined by legal decisions that place parties at the mercy of unregulated lobbies and that give corporations unlimited rights matched by few responsibilities, most beyond reach of legal action. For all practical purposes, the two major American parties are divided by ideologies and historical constituencies that mask their common motivation to serve similar (or identical) economic and financial interests. The party system ties itself to worn-out ideologies that divide the electorate. Polarization is in fact becoming the only strength through which the parties pass their message and promote their agendas. The usual political worn-out lies that become the common truth can survive only by increasing polarization to the point where knee-jerk reactions, mottos, or sound bites replace whole trains of thought. The sheer mention of one emotionally fraught word can trigger predictable reactions, no matter the complexity of an issue. And all other aspects of reality are simply denied.

Financial power, so closely allied to political parties, stands beyond scrutiny. The CEOs of Wall Street, at whose door lies the responsibility for the financial debacles of the last few years, are hailed as heroes, even when they have come out ahead after causing gigantic losses and have benefited from bailouts paid for by taxpayers. They presently continue to operate exactly in the way that caused the problems in the first place. This scenario is acted out on the basis of ideas that come solely from the past.

Such outdated thinking could not be better illustrated than by the last presidential debates (2012), in which climate change was never mentioned, although it is one of the most noteworthy phenomena affecting America and the world at present. We are currently standing between forces that look only at the past (and therefore resort to denial of present issues) and those that have the courage to face the full impact of reality and listen to a future that launches us into uncharted territory. On one hand, in official public discourse we are told that there is only one possibility: to fight until one party prevails over the other. On the other hand, we are saying it is possible to differentiate and integrate contrasting views and to create a future that is far more than the sum of the parts.

The movement called Occupy Wall Street (OWS) has awakened the consciousness of a growing section of the population to the ascendancy of financial powers over the economy and to the screening of Wall Street from all public accountability. It is not surprising that OWS participants refined the art of consensus and applied it in places and situations that were hardly thought possible in the public arena. And this is the real hold that OWS has over the future.

On August 2, 2011, before the OWS occupation of Zuccotti Park, twelve people of the movement's process committee met in New York's Bowling Green Park to decide on a form of consensus decision making to be used in the future OWS general assemblies. And the daring idea was born to operate in assemblies of hundreds through direct democracy. Some among the twelve themselves thought it impossible.[15] Previous practice told them that they could secure the process through spokescouncils to which groups of people would send their representatives, but facilitating a consensus process with a vast, amorphous, and eminently variable crowd of people would present a new challenge. And yet it was not only possible but also predictably replicable. Imagine a crowd randomly converging at a particular point in time in a particular place, and imagine that you can ascertain the will of the people in a succession of situations in which participants and facilitators constantly change. This is exactly what OWS perfected in the elaboration of a mobile and adaptable consensus process, which has roots in early Quaker practice, but which has greatly evolved since.

Referring to the work of the general assembly in Zuccotti Park, Nathan Schneider in the *Occupied Wall Street Journal* writes, "The occupiers are taking their time. When they finally get to consensus on some issue, often after days of trying, the feeling is quite incredible. A mighty cheer fills the plaza. It's hard to describe the experience of being among the hundreds of passionate, rebellious, creative people who are all in agreement about something."[16] These words echo the idea of presencing and the joyful expressions of Scharmer, Jaworski, and Flowers.

Radical innovations often have unsuspected links with our past. The Iroquois Ritual of Condolence has been reborn, first in the twelve steps of Alcoholics Anonymous; then in all subsequent forms of experiential techniques such as nonviolent communication; and culminating in larger and larger group work (social technology and public dialogue and deliberation). Within the new emerging culture, there are no longer clear individual heroes or clear leaders; rather, there are networks in which leadership rises spontaneously and is vested for a time in one group of individuals or another. This kind of leadership gives rise to a true group consciousness that preserves and gives meaning to individuality. This group consciousness will form the ground for the new equality. Individuals who take part in participatory dialogue and decision making bring the experience they derive from their position in the organization, but they otherwise stand as equals. It is through the functional integration of diverging perspectives that Theory U and social technologies of all kinds attain a new synthesis at a higher level in which all needs are honored.

These practices, derived from all forms of American tools for personal growth and group, organizational, and public deliberation, are making it possible to move away from polarization and party politics to decision making that meets the needs of all stakeholders involved. What has been variously called cultural activism, conversational activism, and sacred activism, along with many other names, engages us in the idea that we need to become the change that we want to see in the world. This quiet revolution, moving toward true participation, is reviving humanity's aspiration for the true equality so critical to the American Dream. Democracy can now extend from the periodic expression of the vote to fuller citizen involvement at all levels of the public discourse. It has all the conceivable means for moving from the will of small majorities to a broader seeking of supermajorities or near-consensus. On the other end of a continuum, the American nightmare is making it all too evident that holding on to the past creates an abyss of inequality.

The Awakening to Economic Justice

Chapter 4

What we thought of as isolated pathologies, scarcities of work or hope or security or satisfaction, are not isolated at all; in fact they're intimately related. They're all caused by the same thing, namely the interlocking waste of resources, of money, and of people.

—Amory Lovins

Can America experience an economy that responds to the wishes and core values of its civil society, as well as to government institutions? At present, the economic sector determines our culture and designs its own legislation. The economy has practically bought the political process and subordinated it to its own designs and has all but blotted out the voice of Main Street. A cursory look at what is shown on all major television networks gives the impression that culture is solely what can be advertised and sold. And from the United States this pretended culture sells worldwide. This is the trend at the level of manufactured consensus. And yet global challenges are obliging corporations to set parameters for a complete reevaluation of their way of doing business. And these challenges are being met constructively from a variety of directions.

The Global Economic Horizon: Recognizing the Limits to Growth

Nothing is as it used to be in the global economic landscape of the present; there is no business as usual. Climate change alone imposes a drastic reevaluation of energy and resources consumption, even in the industrialized West. Major corporations are no longer sure that they will have access to basic resources such as water. Nor is energy as abundant or as economically accessible as in the past. In the developing world, supplies of resources are even less reliable. And the challenges to the global environment are still rising.

Globalization, uniting us in a world economy, has also brought us to the unavoidable realization of the finiteness of our planet. Just a few numbers will give the reader an idea of trends: the global number of automobiles has gone from 50 million in 1950 to nearly 800 million in 2008, a sixteenfold increase; 90 percent of computers, televisions, video and audio recorders, and all other electronics end their life cycle in a landfill.[1] The United States alone absorbs some 100 billion tons of raw materials in a year; 90 percent of this sum is the amount that returns as waste product, primarily from extraction and production processes, and 93 percent of plastics in the United States end up as solid refuse in landfills.[2]

The United States is not insulated from global change, even if the media ignore it most of the time. An example: the southeast and southwest regions of our country are already facing the need for rationing and permanent cutbacks in the use of water. In the uncertainty affecting global business, insurance premiums have skyrocketed: there has been a 40 percent increase in Florida, a 20 percent increase in coastal Massachusetts, and a 400 percent increase in some instances of offshore oil rigs.[3]

Adam Smith's vision of the legitimacy of the egoistic motive has led capitalism to just that—an unrestrained pursuit of short-term interest driven solely by economic and financial indicators. Even as we speak, polluting the environment, depleting soils, and undermining long-term capital formation are all considered to be sound capitalistic practices. Not only that, but the accumulation of capital has long been sundered from increased productivity or contribution to the commonwealth. Making money from money is a world unto itself, wholly divorced from economic growth. In order to face the challenges of the future, the economy by necessity will have to be driven away from the motive of unbridled egoistic profit.

Nor have social utopias fared any better worldwide. The reliance of socialism on the hand of the state has not achieved the future it promised for the millions who have had the opportunity to experiment with it. At its best, socialism has been the captive of world capitalism and has offered only a secondary resistance to economic movements it could not control.

Given the reality of a globally interdependent economy, change must be sought within a new paradigm. We need to adopt a new way of thinking about the economic system in relation to its ecological home, a new way of involving all those who have a stake in the economic output, and innovative ways of implementing sustainable economic development that integrates the needs and concerns of public and nonprofit sectors. These three changes can be envisioned by so-called systems thinking, which is a broader collaboration across boundaries; it is a vision that ultimately moves toward the integration of the economy within a larger system, including the political sector and the whole of civil society. All the aspects of the equation are intimately intertwined; none can succeed without the other. In this context, business will no longer be conducted solely for the interests of the shareholders and the financial sector; nor will it be solely regulated and contained through the agency of the state. It will be wholly accountable, both to the political process and to the guiding vision of local, national, and global civil society.

What is needed is a new vision that grows from the grass roots and aggregates the dozens of threads of successful change, no longer on the basis of some abstract theory, but according to a better apprehension of the phenomena that form our economic and social reality. And many visionaries in the United States have been doing and continue to do just that: forming the elements of a growing vision.

Systems Thinking: A New Paradigm

Systems thinking offers an ensemble of ideas and practices based on the belief that the parts that form a system cannot be understood in and of themselves; they can be understood only in context, in the relationships they have with each other and with other systems. Standing in contrast to the Cartesian and Newtonian reductionistic and deterministic worldviews, systems thinking proposes an encompassing and holistic approach.

There has been a slow but steady shift away from mechanistic and materialistic thinking in physics. "The universe begins to look more like a great thought than like a great machine," states Fritjof Capra.[4] Physicists in quantum mechanics are moving away from looking at forces emanating from particles to focusing on the evolving relationships between these particles and how they continuously affect each other. The whole and the part require equal attention. This is a both/and approach rather than either/or. Systems thinking is a new science that applies to the natural, scientific, and social worlds and to business as well.

Whereas Cartesian/Newtonian logic rests on linear relationships between cause and effect, systems thinking focuses on cyclical relationships. A problem can be understood as an imbalance of certain parts in relation to the whole, in an evolving set of relationships. Seeing the economy through such a lens means creating business models that promote not only a corporation's health but also the health of all other systems that interact with it. This is not done in the name of idealism; rather, it is done because of sheer necessity. Individual health (that of the business) truly depends on the health of the whole (that of all internal stakeholders, external stakeholders, the environment, and the culture).

With the adoption of systems thinking, what seems obvious from a theoretical viewpoint has been proven from the perspective of economic business choices. Now that the globe has proved to be finite, practice confirms that there is no trade-off between economy and the environment. Because we are coming to the limits of growth, many now realize that profit and respect for the natural and social environments are tightly interwoven and interdependent. They all increase or suffer together. It is for these reasons that, according to studies, 70 percent of attempts at redesigning businesses failed in the 1990s.[5] And multinational corporations now have an average life expectancy of only forty years.[6]

In organizations, systems consist of people, structures, and processes that work together to make the whole healthy or unhealthy. Parameters to consider are single events, trends, deeper systemic structures or forces, and mental models or assumptions that shape the structures and forces.

- Events: Tangible events are the simplest data to be harvested from the system.

- Patterns/trends: These are determined by looking at what is happening over time. At this stage, stakeholders need to share information to create a more complete picture of reality. A key to seeing holistically is seeing patterns, rather than simply finding causes, merits, or faults in individual factors or players. Patterns are like fractals that reappear at every level of a community or organization.

- Systemic structures or forces: We find these by asking ourselves what the deeper forces are behind the patterns, their origin, and the modality of their formation.

- Mental models: These result from our core beliefs. Examples are nationalism, utopian thinking, and political or religious convictions. Although we may all hold any of these mental models, we are rarely conscious about how they affect our actions. We need to be aware of our assumptions in order to see beyond our blind spots; from an unconscious place, we may be perpetuating the problems we want to resolve.

Comprehensive economic thinking focuses on processes and qualities. It pays attention to patterns, direction, and internal rhythms. It sets the conditions for clear intent, for agreements on how people work together, and for agreements on how they can become better observers, learners, and colleagues. For this comprehensive purpose the widest participation is the most effective organizational strategy—that is, one that includes all internal and external stakeholders. Commitments do not become real until everyone participates in their creation. And the broad premises of systems thinking set the stage for major changes in the way information and communication spread inside the organization.

Information and Communication

Organizational intelligence resides in as many voices as possible, not just in experts or managers. Margaret Wheatley compares the flow of information to a salmon going up the stream.[7] The organization ensures the stream is clear so that many more salmon can get to the source and so that the group can harvest new ideas and projects. This is a view of information as common nourishment, rather than information as power. It is the leadership role to nourish others with truthful and meaningful information. In this way capacity for solutions comes from whatever energy, skill, influence, and wisdom are available—in other words, from any place within the system.

This circulation of information keeps the system able to constantly adapt to new conditions. A free flow of information is necessary for a new orderliness to arise, so that command and control become a thing of the past. This means developing new habits and moving away from looking at negative feedback (deviations from expected outcomes) to focusing on positive feedback that highlights the new and amplifies it. This is an important shift of attention from problems to new resources. Stable systems do not suppress local disturbances; rather, they support them and thus increase the stability of the system. The organization thus prizes natural order over control, and the more freedom there is, the more order will emerge.

Along with information and communication, a special role is played by the promotion of the universal corporate core values of the triple bottom line (people, planet, profit), to which we could add the importance of social processes. Values are the most powerful force of attraction in an organization. And the most important value, by far, is meaning: the idea that you are meant to be there and that your contribution counts. However, new values do not necessarily generate new behaviors. There must be room for self-awareness and reflection and the ability to help each other notice when we tend to return to old behaviors—hence the need for caring feedback. And the extent to which core values reach every place in the community depends on the rise of a new kind of leadership.

The New Leadership

Leadership can be seen as a behavior, not a role, and the need for it can thus be satisfied by different people at different times. The leader is the one who most of all embodies the values of the organization and who is most open to learning the new. The leader is also the one who helps the organization look at itself.

In *Servant Leadership*, Robert Greenleaf advanced the idea that leadership rests on a state of being, not of doing. Joseph Jaworski moves a step further. The leader is the one who decides to make choices that serve life and who can listen to what is wanted in the larger environment.[8] This kind of leadership, usually associated only with individuals such as Gandhi or Martin Luther King, is now available to us all. We need to shift from the idea of exceptional individuals with innate leadership qualities to the practice of bringing forth exceptional leadership qualities in everyone. This is because we are facing the need to create collectively and to collectively shape our destiny. Through this lens, leadership is the ability to shape the future; or as Otto Scharmer would say, it is about sensing what future wants to emerge. By understanding reality differently, we can allow new futures to emerge.

Leadership is about the release of human capacities. Listening is a key element in the ability to inspire others; one could argue it is one of the most important capacities of a leader. "In dialogue you're not building anything, you're allowing the whole that exists to become manifest. It's a deep shift of consciousness away from the notion that parts are primary," states Joseph Jaworski.[9] Coming to the place of true dialogue in a recurring way is a necessity for the life of organizations. It must accompany all the successive phases of their development.

The Power of Networks: Collaborating across Boundaries

Peter Senge sees collaboration as the human face of systems thinking. One cannot work without the other. And collaboration is an art as much as a science. In the new paradigm of change, it is important to allow people free access to each other. Focusing on the quality of relationship means seeing the organization as the place that facilitates energy flows. When there is a goal to be achieved, the attention can go to promoting the energy and supporting the relationships required to achieve a particular outcome.

"Extraordinary change requires building extraordinary relationships, and at some level this requires gathering together diverse people, representing diverse views, so they can speak and listen to one another in new ways," Senge et al. remind us.[10] New, generative dialogues must bring together resources, expertise, key information, people with authority to act, and any stakeholder who will carry out the decisions or be affected by them. In the changing landscape of modern business, it is surprising that organizations would actually expect good results from acting otherwise (unless their success is based on continued political sponsorship and government subsidies).

Centering an organization around the free flow of information and liberating energy where it is present mean that we need to change how we work by building relationships based on trust and reciprocal benefit. For that we need to form emotional connections with the topics, speak from our passion, and build platforms in which all voices can be heard and appreciated. Since this principle applies to all internal as well as external stakeholders, sectors traditionally at odds with each other (e.g., nongovernmental organizations and corporations) are obliged to transform the way they look at the world and to develop skills to see holistically. They thus need to commit to building the capacity to collaborate, which requires investment of time and development of skills, as well as the determination to change the organization and the way people think and work within it.

The new kind of activism helps us not to become cynical in the face of the enormity of our tasks and not to fall into the trap of demonizing those who are on the side of the status quo. This means staying away from both extremes of vitriolic tirades and surface politeness, by moving to empathic listening and generative dialogue, where people can collectively sense what questions really matter for the future. For this purpose, the social technology that we explored in the previous chapter is the foundation stone; new ways of being together and entering into constructive dialogue generate wholly new outcomes, qualitatively different from anything our thinking can conceive when it looks at the past or when it predicts the future according to some ideology or favored lens of interpretation.

Generative dialogue allows us to think not only with the head but also with the heart; balancing advocacy with inquiry is a way to unmask our assumptions and blind spots and receive the new with openness. It's a kind of conversation in which all parties can change perspectives, attitudes, and deeply held beliefs. In following these new ideas and practices, Americans are only furthering a path we have long known. We should remind ourselves of the long processes that were part of the Constitutional Convention, not to mention the months of national education that led to it, and the art of public debate and the subtle balancing of powers that were integral parts of Haudenosaunee (Iroquois) culture.

Some examples

The Sustainable Food Laboratory (Food Lab) is a recent initiative that brings together more than one hundred businesses, government organizations, and nonprofits in the effort to develop sustainable and innovative food systems. All the stakeholders in the system are represented in the initiative. Some examples are nonprofits such as Oxfam, the Nature Conservancy, the World Wildlife Fund, the Rainforest Alliance, and the Kellogg Foundation; governmental organizations from Brazil and the Netherlands; the European Commission; and corporations such as Unilever, General Mills, the International Finance Corporation, Green Mountain Coffee, Organic Valley Cooperative, Rabobank, Sysco, and Costco.[11] Even from this cursory listing, it is not only the great variety of entities but also what many could judge as the sheer impossibility of the intent that is notable. How could one place side by side such different organizations as Oxfam, Unilever, Costco, and the World Wildlife Fund and expect a positive result?

Some of the stated priorities of Food Lab are facilitating connections between small-scale farmers and food companies, increasing access to credit and technical assistance for the producers, and shortening the food chain by strengthening the local food trend.[12] Food Lab incorporates ideas from Otto Scharmer's *Theory U* and expertise from MIT and the Society for Organizational Learning. Although the initiative receives its inspiration in the United States, it is presently global.

When it was started in 2004, Food Lab had a devoted core of forty individuals coming from small organic farming businesses, corporations, global and local nonprofits, cooperatives, and government agencies. Key to the quality of their involvement was the individuals' pledge of forty days of their time over two years to first look at the global food system in a systemic way and then collaboratively envision how to change it.

Gathering such a conglomerate of diverse leaders was the first challenge. The effort would have amounted to nothing without change in the rules of collaboration and creation of a deeper-than-usual commitment to generative dialogue. The first stage was simply listening to in-depth interviews of each team member; this was followed by new learning and capacity-building, through a weeklong introduction to principles of systems thinking. Another week was devoted to a learning journey in rural Brazil. The journey embraced vast extremes: from agribusiness enterprises of sugarcane and soy to small co-ops of coffee and sisal producers, from leading-edge specialty producers to settlements of landless farmworkers. Many of the participants saw a reality they could not have imagined. They talked to people they might never have otherwise encountered in a lifetime, seeing firsthand their life conditions. This experience alone was an example of moving from Cartesian thinking into systems thinking.[13]

Living the preceding experiences together with ample allotments of time allowed participants a chance to exchange their perceptions and views and forge new relationships in a place where each one's experiences and learning had greatly expanded. One NGO member expressed the turning point of the experience in this way: "We are not likely to do one [solve the food problems] without the other [wrestling with one another's experiences and views]. We have gotten to know one another as people, not just 'business people' or 'civil society people'; and to see that we do not have to agree with one another, and that is a good thing."[14]

The Food Lab network and its members presently facilitate new forms of cooperation between multinational food companies and small-scale farmers in Central America and Africa in which the risks and rewards are more evenly distributed between the farmers, the distributors, and everyone in between; they also support the farmers' access to credit and technical assistance. This approach has been extended to bean farmers in Ethiopia, cocoa farmers in Ghana and Cote d'Ivoire, and flower and produce farmers in Kenya and Uganda.[15]

The New Business Models for Sustainable Trading Relationships Project (managed by Food Lab in collaboration with other NGOs), with support from the Unilever/Oxfam partnership, offers access to a new web-based learning platform, Linking Worlds, to support companies and nonprofits that are working on supply chains that are inclusive of small-scale producers in developing countries. The Sustainable Food Lab also collaborates in managing the Cool Farm Institute, which facilitates the collaboration of agricultural producers with multinational food suppliers and retailers. Their goal is to promote agricultural practices that reduce greenhouse gas emissions. Finally, the network "50 in 10" brings together some thirty-six organizations with a ten-year goal of bringing 50 percent of fisheries and the global catch of fish under sustainable management, while increasing economic benefits.[16]

Vision: Committing to Truly Desirable Futures

For a truly sustainable future, we need to move away from the kind of problem solving that addresses overcoming limitations and everything we fear and toward a vision encompassing all desired outcomes. Setting the most ambitious goals is what creates momentum and shift; a zero-emissions goal is the best possible aspiration for the chemical industry, as we will see. Such a goal is not only the most formidable but also the most realistic incentive to rally all stakeholders. And it has been achieved in more than one instance. Fairmount Minerals, one of the largest producers of industrial sand in North America, is an example. The company aligns its mission statement with the ternary of people, planet, and profits. It has used the social technology of Appreciative Inquiry since 1991 in integrating the concerns of all its stakeholders. The company has achieved a remarkable record in preservation of the environment, with a high commitment to air and water quality, as well as to full restoration of its mining sites. From 1991 to 2005, company revenues rose from $48 million to more than $250 million.[17]

To build new leadership networks, much time must be invested in one-on-one and small group conversations. This is a process of iteration, aimed at shaping visions and continually giving new and evolving forms to this cooperation. For that purpose, seeing whole systems is the foundation. Vision is tied to a realistic and encompassing understanding of the place an organization has in the whole.

The vision can never be exact, but vision is what pulls the process forward. It cannot be measured by what it is, but must be measured rather by what it does. And the best vision is closely allied with implementation plans specifying what the organization wants to accomplish and how the group wants to behave together. Vision works together with freedom because people embody that vision individually and differently. Strong vision together with individual freedom is what makes strong organizations, whether these are businesses, nonprofit organizations, or government agencies. And vision with freedom becomes effective when values are conveyed and spoken of at every level of the organization and when a pattern of ethical behavior forms and emerges.

A strong vision is what enables an organization to go through chaotic times. An example is the ambitious Zero to Landfill project of Xerox, from which stemmed a line of green products, developed by engineers of the firm in the late 1990s. The Xerox CEO at that time, Paul Allaire, gave ample latitude to those within the company who had a deep commitment to the environment, so that they could develop a product whose parts could all be reused and/or remanufactured. For its transformational leap, the corporation sought the help of an organization called Terma (now Living Systems) to help its engineers move into a facilitated process that would transform their outlook and connection with nature.

The process started with a two-day individual wilderness experience in New Mexico's high desert. This experience was meant to break loose participants' old ways of thinking, to enable them to operate from a new place, and to help them let go of their conditioning and previous knowledge. For many this was a completely new experience. At the end, the facilitators had the group walk past a landfill where parts of an old Xerox copier had been intentionally placed.

The contrast between the experiences was crucial in allowing something to loosen up and form anew. The engineers were moved in various ways by the experience, and the motto "Zero to Landfill, for the Sake of Our Children" was adopted in 1999. The inspiration of this turning point was used to fuel great creativity and commitment. In practical terms, this meant the start of a new project called Document Center DC 260, which involved some eight hundred engineers, technicians, and management staff and a commitment to people, process, product, and planet guidelines. The copiers that emerged from this transformation of head and heart are now more than 93 percent re-manufacturable and 97 percent recyclable; they are produced in waste-free plants where nothing returns to the landfill. The company estimated that in 2006 more than 122 million pounds of waste were prevented from going to the landfill. The result of this work is now captured by more than 200 patents, and efforts to imitate the results are growing within the industry.[18]

We have just surveyed the elements that govern change and sustainability: systems thinking, collaboration across boundaries, and vision. These are the steps for a larger scale of change, one that moves from a particular business or corporation to the whole of an industrial sector. From here we will look at what economic change can be once the economic sector starts to collaborate with the nonprofit sector to formulate much larger objectives than the so-called bottom line. And from there we will examine tri-sector partnerships, the collaboration between nonprofit, public, and private sectors. These new kinds of collaboration pave the way for the needed shift from a dominant global economy shaping all of society to its needs to a subservient economy responding to the needs and dictates of the body social.

Promoting Change in the Private Sector

Change is already happening from very simple premises. A first step lies in the creation of immediate value by reducing waste, air emissions, and energy use. Great savings can be attained in this manner alone, even without considering the momentum and courage generated by the goals and the credibility earned with all stakeholders.

In 2000, among its goals, Alcoa (the world's leading producer of primary aluminum, fabricated aluminum, and alumina) proposed to reduce greenhouse gas emissions by 25 percent and reduce its waste ending in the landfills by 50 percent by 2010. The company had already met and surpassed the goals by 2003. Buoyed by these successes, the company aimed at zero process-water discharge in its aluminum plants by 2020.[19]

At present, for legitimacy and reputation purposes, companies that want to shift to sustainable policies actively seek qualified NGO input by entering into partnerships with them or hiring their consultants internally. Seeking innovation through the use of renewable energy and resources or offering more secure workplaces can be done much more effectively by collaborating with all stakeholders, especially NGOs and local civic leaders.

With time and practice, some organizations have begun to create what can be called positive-change snowballs. By thinking systemically in the present and toward the future and by reinvesting the profits from better management of resources, companies catalyze self-reinforcing change. Those new investments produce cost-saving benefits themselves. And when one player in the industry can prove the profitability of sustainable choices, others can follow with more confidence, solely on the basis of economic advantage. Once Toyota and Honda showed that hybrid cars could be profitable, other automakers followed suit by either buying those companies' new technology or developing their own.

The experience shows that sustainable planning through systems thinking goes hand in hand with social and environmental sustainability. When this happens, entire sectors naturally tend to form collaborative networks. Examples are the Fair Trade and organic certification standards for coffee and chocolate.

Sustainable corporations are now rising to the top in terms of profitability. A survey conducted by Goldman Sachs in six industrial sectors has surprisingly shown that companies that work systemically (through a combination of environmental, social, and governance strategies) have been surpassing the average stock market performance by 25 percent since 2005; and within a given sector, 72 percent of these show better results than their peers.[20] In fact, consumers are voting with their feet, and brand reputation for social and environmental issues offers companies a competitive edge.

Collaboration between Private and Nonprofit Sectors

Courageous business leaders are now looking for change that can be reached by looking beyond the confines of the business or corporation. In a world of growing complexity and sudden challenges, critical knowledge must be sought outside of the organization itself. NGOs are obvious targets of a sought-after collaboration, since they often specialize in collecting information and know-how about particular aspects that may interest an economic enterprise, be these rare or threatened resources, aspects of sustainability, or cultural trends, for example.

No one organization, government agency, corporation, or nonprofit has a complete grasp of the issues at stake that affect its operations; nor does any one particular entity have the resources, time, authority, or support that it would need locally to integrate the variables of a shifting planetary evolution. Ignoring the dimensions of global change, particularly environmental and social issues, presently places investment capital at risk. Recent experience has shown that even insurance companies and banks now look at environmental liabilities; they assess coverage that the company may need and risks resulting from possible boycott campaigns.

The nonprofit sector plays an important role in exerting positive pressure on corporations. The boycott of Nike (supplier of athletic gear) orchestrated by many NGOs in the 1990s was very effective in bringing a new corporate culture into the corporation; at present Nike has one of the best reputations in the industry. NGOs have realized that they are able to exert pressure to contain negative change, but they cannot affect positive change unless they can create larger alliances, particularly with the private sector.

The World Wildlife Fund (WWF) has entered into a partnership with Coca-Cola to tackle the water problem in a new environment of scarcity that obliges Coke to review its models of growth. Their working together allows them to tackle sustainability challenges in more comprehensive ways, particularly in ways that support the needs of more stakeholders. The availability of water can no longer be taken for granted in the Middle East, large parts of Africa, or Eastern Asia or even in some parts of the United States. The Coke-WWF collaboration has required each party to dispel its respective stereotypical perceptions of the other. The experience brings great organizational learning on both sides, even at the expense of some misperceptions from the public and from the NGO's membership.[21]

Such partnerships are expanding worldwide. Unilever is working in concert with Oxfam in Indonesia to assess the corporation's impact on poverty. Costco is working with Central American farming communities to promote sustainable farming practices. Nike, with the help of local NGOs, is exploring ways for their workers in Thailand to produce their goods at home, rather than in distant factories.[22] At this stage of two-sector collaboration, gains may still be limited, and they may benefit the corporations more than they benefit the environment or local cultures. Issues acquire a different dimension once the collaboration expands to involve all social actors and the three sectors of society simultaneously.

Engaging the Private, Public, and Nonprofit Sectors

We have already briefly mentioned examples of collaborations between two or three sectors in the case of Sustainable Food Labs. We can now turn to an example that is gaining a foothold in our country.

Forty percent of greenhouse gas emissions in the United States come from the consumption generated by all types of buildings (commercial, industrial, and residential), mostly for heating and air conditioning. The building industry is highly competitive and compartmentalized, with lack of dialogue between owners, developers, architects, and contractors. The interest of each group stands at odds with the interest of the others. This often means seeking the least expensive solutions, such as the most affordable heating system or weatherproofing, rather than what is most efficient.

The US Green Building Council (US GBC), the NGO that developed Leadership in Energy and Environmental Design (LEED), tried to find ways through these barriers in the early part of the millennium. Key initiatives came from the work of David Gottfried (a developer), Michael Italiano (an environmental litigator), and Bob Berkebile (founder of the AIA Committee on the Environment, a nonprofit). US GBC and LEED were the result of some ten years of work. LEED now has a certification system for green sustainable building that is used worldwide.

Getting the whole system to collaborate meant bringing together all stakeholders with an interest in construction, members of all three sectors: financiers, engineers, real estate representatives, environmental organizations, the media, and government. And tackling the problem meant enlarging the frame of reference by seeing the whole system. There were strategic conversations that were at times quite unruly, and consensus had to be sought through various iterations. At each turn, action would be taken with a minimal amount of consensus. Ultimately, the encompassing vision paid off.

LEED presently looks at a whole system, not only the use of water, energy, and the materials used for building but also considerations about how the site occupies the land and air and indoor environmental quality. This derived from the realization that architects alone were insufficient to tackle an issue as large as sustainability. A multi-stakeholder approach like the ones we outlined earlier in the chapter was the only way to encompass all issues in a satisfactory fashion.

The formulation of the initial LEED criteria took four years, but the deliberate pace fostered a fruitful collective learning process. It also meant leaving room for everyone's passion to avoid causing centrifugal tensions and splits. The ability of the group to reach such a place of dialogue could be fostered only through carefully crafted dialogue and decision-making processes in which mutual relationships were nurtured and deepened.

After LEED's system was established, the number of registrations grew from 635 buildings in 2002 to more than 7,500 worldwide by mid-2007.[23] Moreover, LEED is becoming an industry norm and is being adopted by a growing number of cities such as Atlanta, Boston, Chicago, San Francisco, Houston, and Seattle.[24] By 2008, 715 US cities had committed to reducing greenhouse emissions.[25]

As experience has increased, the building cost of satisfying LEED standards has fallen; in 2008 it cost only 2 percent more to build a green, efficient building than to build a standard building. In the same year, energy savings from these buildings had climbed from an initial 25 percent to more than 70 percent.[26] At present there is even talk about living buildings, which are capable of capturing and producing surplus energy and more clean water than they use. The criteria for defining such buildings include ecological methods for purifying water, treating waste, and heating and cooling the building. These methods may include living machine technology, which uses plants to purify and clean the air, water, and waste.[27]

The results in the construction sector are showing another encouraging trend when businesses collaborate to harvest the fruits of innovation as well as to share research results. The benefits of this work are now applied to retrofitting older buildings. LEED has set a good example with an effective management commons, in which countless developers, architects, and contractors have a stake in using and continuously improving the system by sharing their own best practices, breakthroughs, and innovations and in introducing more comprehensive and demanding standards.

Integrated Tri-Sector Community Development

We will now turn to examples of tri-sector partnerships in community development. The first ones come from the early days of the already-mentioned Institute for Cultural Affairs (ICA), which goes to show that systems thinking has long been part of American reality. What Peter Senge and Otto Scharmer are offering in their new views of economic development has long been promoted by earlier American pioneers. This look backward in time points to ideas that are still far into the future. They can inspire our present.

At the heart of ICA's development success was a new educational model. The whole-systems curriculum presented cutting-edge ideas in cultural disciplines and social structures; it focused on internally consistent models, able to match reality on the ground. Of a total of twelve courses, six were theoretical, and six practical. Academic and practical work went hand in hand. The overall concern was to address

- reductionism and fashions of the moment in curriculum designs,
- separation of all areas of knowledge from life questions, and
- the divide between sciences and humanities.

Courses in science were paired with the humanities: psychology and art; science and philosophy, sociology and history. The same model was used from preschool to adult education, and it addressed both methodology and "final meanings" grounding the content in the lives of the learners. Following were some of the studies:

- Religious Studies I: twentieth-century theology of Bultmann, Bonhoffer, Tillich, Niebuhr, and others
- Twentieth-century cultural revolution
- Imaginal education consisting of images of education and new methods for teaching
- Intellectual methods: conversational method, charting method, seminar method, lecture building and presentation methods, and corporate writing
- Social methods: facilitation methods such as workshop method, action planning, and strategic planning
- Personal growth methods (motivational studies): solitary reflection, depth conversations, other-world mythology, studies of classical spiritual writers (psalmist, Theresa of Avila, John of the Cross) and modern spiritual authors (Hermann Hesse, Nikos Kazanzakis, Joseph Campbell).[28]

This curriculum further evolved in the 1970s and 1980s to incorporate the best that culture could offer then. In the 1970s was added the interfaith aspect: studies of the long night of the soul through Sufis, Lao Tzu, Chuang Tzu, and Castaneda; the 1980s saw the addition of the work of Jean Houston and Willis Harman, visualization techniques, neurolinguistic programming, and so on. In 1965 the first annual Summer Research Assembly took place, inaugurating the global research assemblies, which gathered up to a thousand people from all over the world in one site. The research assemblies continued until the mid-1980s.[29]

The preceding comprehensive systems-thinking approach was tried out in its early stages in the so-called Fifth City and later on in ICA's worldwide project of human development.

Fifth City

In 1963 a nucleus of seven families, determined to put the new ideas to the test, moved to a ghetto neighborhood of the West Side of Chicago that encompassed a total of ten blocks, populated predominantly by African Americans. The neighborhood was called Fifth City because of the recognized four categories of cities, from which it wanted to distinguish itself: downtown, inner city, suburb, and rural. The fifth was a decisional city.

The Ecumenical Institute (later Institute for Cultural Affairs) itself was in the heart of that area. The newcomers approached the local population with door-to-door interviews and neighborhood meetings, through which they gained an overall view of the residents' main concerns, and with them, they began to design strategies of intervention. This comprehensive approach covered many social issues such as childhood education; programs for youth, adults, and elders; health care; housing; and economic revitalization. The interviewers uncovered more than five thousand problems and categorized them into economic, political, and cultural issues.

Fifth City used all of the new curriculum design of the comprehensive educational method from its beginning. These were some of the approaches:

- Seeing poverty as a manifestation of the cultural level and offering cultural programs for the neighborhood.
- Education formulating a new image of self through poetry, drama, and art.
- Reaching out to teenage gang members and to teenagers in general through a fifteen-week course; this was considered important for the future leadership of Fifth City.
- Moving eighteen suburban families, both black and white, back into the city, among them a doctor and a businessman, encouraging redevelopment from within.
- Remodeling a vacant house, which became a symbol for the neighborhood.
- Calling on college volunteers.[30]

In four years Fifth City trained some 450 people in new job development positions. It also started rehabilitating apartments and a community center, opened a shopping center hosting five businesses, and inaugurated an auto service center and a car wash. In addition, Fifth City owned equipment with which it could communally improve the infrastructure and landscape.[31]

All of the coordinated activity attracted the new Bethany Hospital and the CTA bus garage for a total of $40 million in investment. The two entities employed over a thousand people in the neighborhoods. Many partnerships were formed between Fifth City and businesses, with local government, and with other nonprofit organizations.

In 1968, at the death of Martin Luther King Jr., the neighborhood was affected by the riots, and they started to rebuild immediately. In commemoration of the events, they built the Iron Man sculpture just in the center of Fifth City.

Worldwide Community Development

After 1975, demonstration community projects patterned after Fifth City were established worldwide, one in every time zone, twenty-four in all. The projects were selected on the basis of high accessibility to all and their ability to be pioneers in economic, social, and cultural renewal, tackling all local issues and involving all local stakeholders. Often, an initial project would spur replication in neighboring communities. Soon there were about three hundred projects started in twenty-five nations.[32]

What was unique to all projects was the idea of bringing together all stakeholders of the community, voluntary consultants from the public and private sectors, and ICA staff, who together designed a comprehensive four-year plan of local development. Each development project began with a weeklong conference with all aforementioned stakeholders, and from this "consult" came out a plan for comprehensive local development. After the event ICA left an average of three couples from its staff in the community to teach the methods of community development and offer leadership trainings for about four years. The community continued its own development independently after this deadline.

The institute was invited to begin similar projects in Australia and the Marshall Islands. In India this was carried out in a group of 232 villages in the Maharashtra state, and the experiment was known as the "New Village Movement." In Kenya, a larger project involved up to a thousand villages. It was seeded by the initial, successful experiment in Kawangware, a slum near Nairobi. Smaller projects were started in the Philippines and Indonesia.

Summing Up

Naturally, the idea of bringing together the three sectors is in its infancy. Such partnerships must overcome not only natural inertia but also the difficulty of bridging cultures that speak widely different languages and that have very different aims. This kind of bridging is truly a new social pursuit. More than anything else, it is the way beyond the false alternatives of the power of the market and Wall Street on one hand and social change mandated through the agency of the state on the other hand. Sector collaboration promises change on the sound basis of well-understood social phenomena: systems thinking, generative conversations, sound collaboration, weakening of social stereotypes, and so forth.

Through wider collaboration of civil society, public sectors, and private sectors, the economy can address all aspects of sustainability. When unbridled economic pursuit is put in check by cultural mandates and political restrictions, the concerns of all stakeholders, internal and external to the business sector, will be considered. The result will be sustainability at ecological and economic levels. The examples of LEED and ICA are only a beginning of what is possible. We have, however, more to learn from the work of ICA and other actors we have heard from so far. We can now assemble the parts of the edifice and look at cultural renewal and social change from a holistic and integrated perspective. We will take a peak at a vision that is not only organic but also naturally mobile. It requires our imagination and willingness to engage and cannot be put forth in the same way one would an ideology or a party platform.

Chapter 5
A Vision of the Larger
Dimension of Social Change

e have been presenting parts of a puzzle, aspects of the American Dream, and facets of the social dilemma we are facing as Americans. The American Dream speaks of individual freedom ("land of the free"); of broad equality among all, irrespective of cultural, religious, or racial backgrounds, personal lifestyles, and so on ("all men are created equal"); and of equal opportunity for all to make the living they aspire to and satisfy their economic needs ("land of opportunity"). Let us look at this more closely, reviewing what has been brought forth.

"Freedom" is the term in this equation that poses the greatest challenge to our minds. Freedom cannot be equated with the right to do as one pleases, since this prerogative automatically undermines other people's freedom. In this book we have discerned in freedom everything that affirms and upholds the essence of the human being and extends new understanding to individuality, everything that contributes to a new culture where more of the human experience finds its place. A new culture will do everything to support individual freedom, and from the contributions of free individuals, it will renew itself further.

With the terms "equality" and "democracy," we have recognized not just everything that allows equal protection of the law but also fuller participation in the political process beyond the vote. In their processes, American businesses, nonprofits, and community development organizations are making the transition from narrow majorities to the seeking of supermajorities and even consensus; this is a growing reality, something that can be achieved if the political will is present. This transition has also been tried successfully at the local political level.

With "economic justice," we are calling for the subordination of the economy to the ideas of ecological, cultural, and social sustainability at the antipodes of the present state of affairs. This consists of turning upside down the present reality that corporations are individuals and accountable to none. The economy will be ecologically sustainable and socially just only when it is subordinated to a cultural project carried by civil society and restrained by political constraints. When civil society has the strength to carry forward a project of society that is truly independent from the state and the economic sector, then the corporations will have to bow to a force that is stronger than their own. When all stakeholders are present in economic determinations, sustainability and economic justice will become a common ground from which everything will derive. Economy will no longer be the engine of societal development; it will be subordinated to human needs, which is its more natural function.

The preceding ideas can still appear as a disjointed collection of insights. Where is the glue that puts them all together? Where are the pioneer thinkers who are paving the way to a new integration of ideas? Where is that systems thinking that makes of the whole more than the sum of the parts? Such thinking has existed from the 1970s to the present. We will turn now to two examples, spanning four decades.

A New Role for Culture

Not only did the Ecumenical Order, or Institute for Cultural Affairs, effect the complete renewal of the Chicago ghetto known as Fifth City; many other development projects were carried out worldwide, which were adapted to all the aspects of the local culture. What made all of this possible was a key event that took place in the early 1970s and molded the vision of ICA. In 1971 the Order: Ecumenical—introduced in chapter 2—conducted a worldwide global research project, surveying more than one thousand books concerning the social question. It was a worldwide study involving about one thousand individuals worldwide. Conversations were guided by the facilitative processes that are known by the designation "Technology of Participation." The global research produced an insight that—as naïve as it may appear at first reading—was actually a major breakthrough: that culture could be added on an equal footing to politics and the economy, as a third, independent area of society. From this breakthrough were born the "social process triangles," of which more will be said presently.[1] The independent role of culture in the social arena was the key contribution of the model. The new emphasis on culture and the shift away from the original religious focus led to the organization's adoption of its new name—Institute for Cultural Affairs—in 1973.

The social question, ICA argued, can be articulated through the contribution of the economic, political, and cultural commonalities. These three major processes of society take their impulse from three basic drives found in all humans and in all societies. The first is the *drive for survival, resources, livelihood, and money* (the economic dimension of life); without it there can be no decision making and no consciousness. The second is the *drive for order*, the drive for the organization of society through law-making and law-enforcing bodies so that there is security and justice for all (the political dimension of society). Third is the *drive for meaning* (the cultural component of society), which bestows significance on both the economic and the political dimensions of society.[2] The interrelationship between the three commonalities was conceived thus:

> To be a social human being is to be inexorably involved in issues of sustenance and survival (economic); of ordering and organizing society to overcome chaos (political); and of education, family, and community, and the celebration of life and death (cultural). These three, together with all the particular processes that make them up, create the whole system that we call society, or the social process. Because the social process is systemic, any malfunction in any one part will reverberate through the whole system. The same goes for the good things going on in any one part. In addition, if there is not some kind of basic balance between the three major processes, the whole social process suffers.[3]

Regarding the state of balance or imbalance of the system, these were some of the conclusions of the research:

The ideal (rarely found) is a balanced tension between the economic, the political, and the cultural. When this happens, society is in a healthy state. When these three processes of society are not held in balance, society gets sick. When we are deprived of the means of adequate livelihood, political chaos and rioting can result. When we are deprived of participation in the political process, our livelihood is likely to suffer while masters grow rich on the resources denied us. When our culture is taken away from us, we easily become political and economic victims, or find our lives devoid of meaning.[4]

ICA used triangles as a convenient symbol for showing the connections between the three sectors. The first-level triangle (Figure 5.1) quite simply introduces the reality of the three commonalities, but it also brings out something more than the obvious.

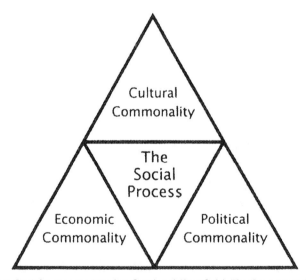

Figure 5.1: Social process triangles, first level (Stanfield, *The Courage to Lead*, 149).

In this triangle we can see the relationships of three parts

- Foundational (economic): without it the other two cannot go on.
- Ordering or organizational function (political): "the communal pole, which pertains to the relationship of power

and decision-making in the midst of any social group"; it "counteracts people's fundamental tendency to destroy each other, by creating a social contract."

- Sustaining, meaning-giver (cultural): "this is the dynamic which dramatizes the uniquely human in the triangle; it is the spirit which makes participation in the social process worthwhile. This is the arena of the symbols, style, and stories which give significance to the whole."[5]

The placement of the cultural arena at the top of the triangle reveals the determining place it occupies in relation to the other two areas. This perspective offers a counterweight to the present societal illness of an economic system run amok, which is causing havoc in the cultural and political sectors.

Each of the three processes creates, sustains, and limits the other two. Each of the three processes can be broken into its components at deeper levels, and there one would find again the tension between a foundational process (economic component) at the bottom left; a connecting process (political component) at the bottom right; and an informing process (cultural component) at the top.

The first-level triangles, if refined into triangles of higher orders and specificity, can be applied at every level from the community to the national and international levels. There are triangles from the first to the sixth level of detail; the second level is given in Figure 5.2. These illustrations allow us to place any of the smaller processes in society into a comprehensive context, showing how they are connected to the other areas of the social organism, enabling us to assess the health or imbalance of any given social unit. They can offer visualizations of what patterns are at play in a particular situation, thus throwing light on where the leverage points of the whole system are. If action is taken at these points, positive effects will ripple throughout the system. This approach explains the successes that ICA experienced in the United States and worldwide. From Figure 5.2 we can see how each segment of the triangle repeats the threefold ordering.

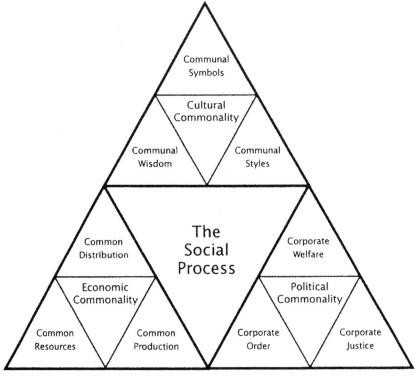

Figure 5.2: Social process triangles, second level (Stanfield, *The Courage to Lead*, 149).

At the second level in the economy, we have resources (economic component); production (political component); and distribution (the cultural component). The same tri-partition is true for the political commonality and the cultural commonality. The analysis of the triangles can be applied to our form of government. At the third level of the political commonality, in the political side of the triangle we find what corresponds to the US national government. When we further break down this side of the triangle, we find executive (economic component), legislative (political component), and judicial (cultural component).

The truly groundbreaking work of ICA condenses everything that has been brought out in this book. ICA's work is a remarkable illustration of the interrelatedness of the processes of change, which culminate in an articulate vision of the primacy of culture, and of the necessity of a conscious collaboration between the three sectors.

In the developments that followed the birth of the social process triangles, ICA also set new precedents. Together with many practicing consultants, it started the International Association of Facilitators and set up a number of international conferences, such as Our Common Future in an Environment of Change (Taipei, 1990); Exploring the Great Transition to Our One World (Prague, 1992); and the Rise of Civil Society in the 21st Century (Cairo, 1996).[6] Thus, a 1996 conference on civil society heralded the role that civil society played in its coming to birth at the global level in the events around the 1999 WTO conference in Seattle.

At present, restoring the American Dream means a return to the primacy of culture and civil society over economy and corporations, which shackle the political process. Forty years after ICA talked about the state of balance that it sought to achieve between the three sectors, the United States has now become a textbook case of what extreme social imbalances look like. At the root of this colossal dysfunction lies our economic inequality, which is the highest among all industrial nations. In 2011, 42.7 percent of the national wealth was concentrated in the hands of the richest 1 percent; the bottom 80 percent shared a meager 7 percent of the remainder.

The consequences ray out from this simple root cause in all directions, finally affecting us even in our physical well-being. In order to protect this inequality of wealth, the United States devotes almost a quarter of its labor force to security, whether through the military, worldwide military contractors, the police, prisons, or specialized security forces. Not surprisingly, the United States harbors the highest per capita prison population in the world, with seven million people incarcerated in 2007, an estimated 23.5 percent of the world's reported prison population. The costs of this vast enterprise reach a staggering $60 billion per year. The American defense budget nearly equals that of all other nations in the world combined. That is easy to believe since the United States maintains some 710 military bases, spread over some eighty countries. Finally, as a predictable consequence, the United States ranks only forty-eighth in terms of individual longevity, yet it spends practically double what most all other countries spend on health care; the per capita number averaged $2,966 in all OECD (Organization for

Economic Cooperation and Development) countries in 2007, compared to $7,600 in the United States.[7]

We will now turn to a more recent vision of social development driven from culture. It comes from the work of Otto Scharmer. His contribution to the idea of social renewal has been highlighted in a new understanding of what is possible with social processes of facilitation and decision making and the change process of the so-called U. Scharmer has gone further in bringing the parts to a holistic integration. We turn here to his vision of the integration of a new economy within a new social project.

A Vision for the New Economy

The American Revolution marked an important moment in the evolution of social compacts. America was born out of a strong cultural impulse that made possible the writing of documents such as the Declaration of Independence and the Bill of Rights. That impulse brought the cultural transition from the divine rights of kings to the primacy and sovereignty of the individual. The original thrust receded in time, and now we can rightly call it a dream, no longer aware of itself.

In terms of the social process triangles, America was born as a response to colonialism and to European monarchies, which had enshrined the alignment of the political sphere with the economic process. That silent agreement provided the foundation for financial monopolies that made colonialism an economic reality. The American form of government repudiated the primacy of the economy and established the political and economic arenas side by side. In addition, cultural power acquired some measure of autonomy through the Bill of Rights, through the power of the Supreme Court to uphold individual rights against the tyranny of majorities, and through the strength of cultural institutions.

Over time in the history of the nation, the three sectors started to negotiate their mutual interactions. A major step along the way, according to Otto Scharmer, was the New Deal of 1933–1936. At this stage, the public and the private sectors had differentiated; the growing civic sector had become visible because of the proliferation of NGOs. America entered a state that Otto Scharmer calls "stakeholder capitalism."[8] At this stage the externalities (economic, environmental, and cultural) that are generated from an unbridled economy are addressed and tempered through contractual agreements and continuous negotiations. These include wealth redistribution (progressive taxation), social security, trade unions, environmental legislation and regulations, subsidies, welfare programs, and so forth. The equilibrium within the system can be precarious and often leads to persistent antagonism or even open conflict. Nor is the system able to fully apprehend the living dimension of the social system and its interaction with the natural environment or the international economy.

The ideology at the stage of stakeholder capitalism integrates market and government; that approach still worked to a degree as long as the economy could be approached within national boundaries. However, the global economy, which has grown over the centuries, and massive ecological disruptions have changed the social discourse. The present system of negotiations and accommodations fails to address rising global challenges, such as peak oil, climate change, and growing wealth disparity. In addition, this approach favors the strongest interest groups and corporate lobbies, and in times of crisis, it tends to accelerate all disparities. The wealthy, large corporations and major polluters, the investment banks, and all other organized special interests reap all the benefits, while passing the externalities on to the taxpayer and eroding or encroaching upon the commons. Those who cannot organize with equal ease (e.g., the poor, the consumers), because they either are too diffuse or simply lack the means, do not sit at the negotiating table as equals. Neither do future generations.

The 1980s and 1990s, culminating in the 1999 repeal of the Glass-Steagall Act—removing the last effective regulations over the stock market—turned the clock backward toward a purer market economy, in which big business dictates its wishes to the political arena, and civil society is altogether ignored. At present the country is deeply divided between advocates of a return to unbridled market liberalization (conservative Republicans) on one hand and advocates of a reengineering of the welfare state (liberals) on the other. The left-versus-right rift, Scharmer reminds us, represents the thought of the eighteenth and nineteenth centuries, as contrasted with that of the twentieth century. Both fail to include the future. Unfortunately, the most regressive forces now seem to be gaining the upper hand. Will we have enough future-minded visionaries to propel us into a new dream? This book has been advocating completely new developments, not a return to the past—not the past of the unbridled industrial revolution or the past of a welfare state, which has been outgrown by the imperatives of economic globalization and global ecological challenges.

Conclusions

*T*he American Dream was an audacious departure from the past; it was a jump into the unknown, into the future that some great minds and hearts were hearing faintly. The dream trusted visionaries against all odds, when the sober "voices of reason" could not foresee any chance of success. It was a generous vision of the human being that propelled the dream. The dream upheld the value of the individual at a time when it was considered a subject to be ruled by the wiser guidance of kings. Trusting individuality raised suspicions of all sorts; it could not work. America tried for two centuries the experiment that upheld the idea of individual freedom and equality under the law. And the dream reached further in the hope of being the land of opportunity, thought it is true that what this meant was unclear from the very start.

The dream was not perfect. Important issues had not been resolved: What would happen with slavery was not clear; how could it fade out? Nor was the whole financial question addressed. How would money be issued? And by whom? Decades and centuries of struggle followed surrounding these two major issues and others. The dream wore out, the dream receded, and the nightmare entered its place. America has reached a place of exhaustion. Its culture is threatened. Its democracy no longer represents the people of the nation, and corporations buy the political process and set its tone and content. Growing poverty and wealth disparity are the only possible and logical outcomes.

We are at a place of new beginnings, like 250 years ago. If there is to be a new dream, it will have to answer the call of the future and let outworn ideologies die. The great contrast of our time is no longer between right and left, between capitalism and socialism and all the variations that have evolved from them. The real choice lies between what clings to a past that has been defeated and disproved in the last centuries and a vision that has grown steadily under the surface and strives for its day under the sun. The latter is a proposition that has matured and passed many a test in the last forty to fifty years; it is no longer a wild guess, a speculation. We can no longer tinker and reform; a massive overhaul is needed, one that is based on a comprehensive vision. Martin Luther King and Occupy Wall Street have given us a glimmer of what this may look like.

America can truly encompass seemingly divergent ideals. It can be "the land of the free," the land where "all [human beings] are created equal," and the "land of opportunity." None of these aims need be sacrificed to the others. Integrating them is the challenge. This book has wanted to show that not only is this possible, but it seems to be the only way forward.

America can live in the past of denial or in the future of a bold vision. Denial is becoming commonplace. Two examples illustrate this. The last thirty years have brought us two catastrophes that were "impossible": Chernobyl and Fukushima. Volumes of denial had preceded the obvious. When the catastrophes happened, all the dikes of denial ruptured. Denial that no longer works is followed by silence about the obvious and by deepening secrecy.

Our present administration came to power buoyed by a great wave of hope for the precedent of an African American president. In the early days we heard the promise of greater transparency in government. Many were already sobered within a few months of the change of the guard, and things have become alarmingly clear as time has passed. Not only has this administration been more aggressive against all whistleblowers than all previous administrations combined; it has also spent considerable time and resources denying the obvious. When Edward Snowden's revelations started to trickle, we heard reassuring addresses at all levels of the administration that something of the sort was simply not possible, or in any case very limited and submitted to all kinds of reasonable safeguards. Nobody should worry. After it became clear that Americans and nations worldwide were being monitored on a massive scale and lied to on a routine basis, official silence took the place of denial. As if on a signal from above, Edward Snowden has simply ceased to exist for the corporate press. Has he become just too obvious for denial to have its effect?

Let us look at another significant and eloquent example of denial leading to secrecy and seizure of power: the projected finalizing of the Trans-Pacific Partnership (TPP). The United States and twelve Pacific Rim nations have been crafting the TPP "trade agreement" behind closed doors. Had it not been for WikiLeaks' posting of the ninety-five-page draft of the projected agreements, the American citizen would not know about truly encompassing provisions of law relating to patents, copyright, trademarks, and industrial design, devised behind the American citizen's back, in circumvention of all democratic process. American sociopolitical reality would have been, and still may be, permanently altered at the stroke of a pen, with only the pretense of a democratic process.

The highly secretive trade deal would amount to some 40 percent of the global economy. In November 2014 trade ministers of the twelve countries were still meeting in Beijing to continue negotiations. And President Obama originally wished to expedite passage of the TPP legislation before the end of the year and request from Congress legislation granting the executive "fast-track authority."[1]

Among many of its sweeping provisions, the TPP proposes banning the Buy America, Buy Local policies awarded to the federal government and states. But that is not all: of the agreement's twenty-nine chapters, the great majority are not about trade.

For what concerns trade, the TPP lines the pockets of companies such as Monsanto, which would extend its monopoly rights through its genetic patents over wheat and corn; Walt Disney, which would be able to criminally prosecute people for downloading films; and Big Pharma, which would increase the duration of patents and reap windfall profits by increasing medicine prices. Naturally, TPP would ease financial regulation on big banks. And finally, it would limit Internet freedom, after Congress failed to pass the Stop Online Piracy Act, SOPA. In other words, TPP is a back door to legislation that cannot be achieved democratically in the United States.

Not surprisingly, the TPP would have two strong enforcement mechanisms. If the United States, for instance, were to continue the Buy American policy, and states or communities continued the Buy Local policies, both would find themselves in violation of TPP provisions. Third-party countries, deeming themselves affected, could sue the United States in a TPP tribunal and impose trade sanctions or fines. A second option contemplates that TPP provisions could be enforced directly by corporations, which would call for the US government to compensate them for violations of the agreements, on the basis that these violations undermined their expected future profits.

Consider that all of this was meant to remain secret. And this is only the first layer. Fast-tracking adds the second layer of secrecy. Through this seldom-used procedure, Congress delegates its authority over trade (and other matters) to the president. Not only does the commander in chief write legislation; what he writes into law also gets a guaranteed ninety-day vote with no amendments. This procedure has been used only sixteen times in US history, but not surprisingly both for the NAFTA agreements and for the World Trade Organization.

The state of denial and secrecy, only two small examples of which have been offered, points to the cultural vacuum that has taken hold of the land. Fortunately, it is not the only cultural reality. Two cultures live, as if side by side. An emerging culture is painting broad new brushstrokes to show a fuller image of the human being, American and global. The two cultures are struggling against each other, and the battle takes place within every one of us. The new vision that is being born takes courage, and nobody can carry it at every moment without faltering. Carrying the new vision means asking ourselves the important questions that all civilizations have asked themselves if they wanted to flourish: What is the human being? What is the meaning of this life on earth? What is the place of the human being in the universe? In the end does who we are and what we do really matter?

The two cultures will trace completely antithetical pictures. On one hand, the movement of denial and secrecy can culminate only in total power and the destructive tendencies that go with it: more wars, more environmental degradation, more disregard for individual freedoms. It is not something we need to speculate about. It is the reality spreading and emerging all around us. On the other hand, a new culture will have to be completely nonviolent, inclusive, and transparent. It will have to build on what gives life to the essence of individuality, to what is life-affirming for the planet. It can certainly stand its ground against everything that continues outworn past trends. It can overwhelm its adversary, not fight it, for the latter would mean strengthening the habits of the past.

We need a new narrative of what it means to be human. We have shown how new answers have come from audacious individuals—from people like Emerson, Bill Wilson, and Elisabeth Kübler-Ross, but also from Martin Luther King Jr. and many others. They have wrested meaning from the edge of the abyss; they are cultural heroes. And only a nation that can offer its individuals meaning can be the land of the free.

The contributions of the aforementioned cultural heroes cannot be carried yet by political institutions. The search for meaning needs to take place in our schools, in our institutions of learning, in the sciences, in the arts, in religion and spirituality. New sources of meaning naturally emerge from the activities of civil society, the network of organizations that are now best known as NGOs. A strong culture must find a place of its own, independent from the political discourse or the dictates of business.

America can be once more the land of the free. Once again, we need to trust the visionaries and look to the future. These visionaries are showing that science and religion can be reconciled, that the human being can be endowed with new meaning without having to draw from dogma or traditions of the past. The foundations have been built. Others will erect the new buildings of a new culture. We may all feel that more needs to happen, but there is already a very promising start.

A culture that is dying can gain time and new oxygen only by setting individuals against individuals. Today, this is visible in the degree of polarization in American politics. Important and fundamental questions are addressed with the simplest of political arguments. Lines are drawn in the sand, and nobody can stand close to them, or step over them, to contemplate original answers. There is no time to decide.

"You are with us or against us" is a constant rallying cry. Americans are happily segregating themselves from each other and doing the dirty work for the powers that be. Members of the 1 percent can preserve their power only if they can divide and set the 99 percent against each other. The more we polarize public opinion, the harder it will be to set new conditions for a future political discourse. The future will come only from diversity, inclusion, and integration of all voices. It is not a future we can predict, but rather one that we have to learn to discern in our hearts and trust in our minds.

Here, too, two visions of the future prevail. The first one has a long history. And it has had its glory too. The democracy of "one person, one vote" was extremely significant when the voices of individuals needed to emerge as if out of the void. It was important for decades and centuries, until it ceased to make a difference. Today, this is far too little and far too dangerous. It is extremely easy to control the public debate, to divide and control, to foster mutual demonizing and spread the idea that one's hopes can be reached only through victory and at the expense of someone else, or the idea that weak compromises are all that we can ever hope for in the best of worlds. Accepting this false dilemma means repeating trends from the past that have not worked for quite some time and can no longer work.

Today, democracy and participation mean so much more than voting every now and then. Once again, we can turn to those who are already walking into the future, who have, so to say, already tried it and mapped it out. Today we can participate in public decision making on a more regular basis and move from simple majorities to supermajorities and near-consensus. There are innumerable social tools for moving from weak compromise to strong consensus. Social technology offers us examples after example: consensus decision making, World Café, Appreciative Inquiry, Technology of Participation, Open Space Technology, and so on. These approaches have been used in organizations of all kinds; in corporations, communities, and social networks; and in local politics. And new ideas of dialogue and deliberation have also been boldly applied to problems of local governance, or envisioned at the state and national levels. Political change can happen regardless of ideological divides, when people are engaged in processes of decision making that look at them as individuals expressing legitimate needs and aspirations, rather than as representatives of one ideology or another. It has long been established that the only lasting change comes from integrating all perspectives, hearing everybody, and giving everybody a say in the search for solutions. It is actually a surprise that we may expect results when ready-made ideas or quick solutions are forced against a sizable minority.

Through social technology and public deliberation, the stage has been set for a paradigm shift in the way organizations and communities of all sorts and purposes can co-create viable futures and address the most daunting challenges that the planet faces. What seemed impossible yesterday can be done today. Zero emissions is the best goal for a chemical corporation. It is the one that mobilizes the most energy for the goal. Ecological and economic sustainability, social justice, and respect for all cultures are the only goals worth pursuing. Nobody in their right mind will invest the considerable amount of time and energy needed only to reach weak compromises on minor issues.

Obviously, if the matters were this simple, we could just expect legislation that enforces this state of affairs soon. But here is the rub: all great ideas correspond to a paradigm shift. When we embrace such a momentous proposition, we are already embarking on a path of personal transformation, exhilarating and frightening at the same time. Who doesn't resist change? It is obviously through education and self-education that we can reach these goals. It is by being willing to try, fail, and try again.

America can become anew the land where all human beings are created equal. We know this to be a far cry in the present. But change will not be legislated. It will be won in each human heart, with effort. Only when this personal change reaches a certain momentum will legislative change be able to follow.

Last, all Americans yearn to live in the land of opportunity. They yearn for economic justice, for the just retribution for their efforts, for a place where all contributions to society can give individuals their just rewards. They yearn for an economy that has its place, and no more than its place, in the arena of society.

And an important change needs to happen. The economy cannot drive the search for meaning, as it is doing in the present. When this happens, immense misery is the only predictable result, and America has spread this misery beyond its own borders. America has spread worldwide a model that is not sustainable, that cannot offer justice or meaning. Here is where the greatest change needs to occur. Economy, which has been turned into a new idol and placed first and foremost, needs to return to last. Business is really in its place when it serves a greater ideal, when it is subordinated to a project of society and to the desires of the citizenship.

We can turn once more to visionaries who have walked the future before their fellow human beings. Sustainability, social justice, freedom, and respect for all cultures are possible when we see the whole, above the parts. The economy needs to be seen in relation to the larger issues of society and subordinated to them. Successful sustainable development has been promoted over the last forty to fifty years, when the economy has been seen under the holistic lens of systems thinking or other, similar approaches. Integrating the economy with all stakeholders that benefit from it, or are made to suffer from it, will be the way of the future. Once again, this is something that we need to approach and learn. There will be much trial and error.

Distinct cultures need to learn to talk to each other. Political agencies speak one language; corporations, another one; and NGOs, yet another one. The future can emerge only when the three sectors start talking to each other and understand that a vision of the whole society can come only from integrating its major players. Such a high-level dialogue will actually be much harder than fighting to oppose what we don't like. But is there really an alternative?

A dream can be reborn when enough people decide to dream the new together, when they are willing to sail into the future and abandon the safe shore of what they already know, when they are willing to be audacious as well as uncomfortable, when they set their shoulders to the wheel and are willing to embark on personal change as much as demand social change. America can be the land of opportunity again, but first it needs to be the land of the free and the land where all are equal.

Chapter 1

1) http://wwf.panda.org/about_our_earth/all_publications/living_planet_report/living_planet_index2/.

2) "World Wildlife Fund, Living Planet Report 2012, Biodiversity, Biocapacity and Better Choices," http://d2ouvy59p0dg6k.cloudfront.net/downloads/1_lpr_2012_online_full_size_single_pages_final_120516.pdf, 100.

3) Paul McCaffrey, ed., *Global Climate Change*, Reference Shelf, vol. 78, no. 1 (New York: H. W. Wilson, 2006), 10.

4) McCaffrey, *Global Climate Change*, 11.

5) McCaffrey, *Global Climate Change*, 11.

6) Otto Scharmer and Katrin Kaufer, *Leading from the Emerging Future: From Ego-System to Eco-System Economies* (San Francisco: Berrett-Koehler, 2013), 9.

7) Emmanuel Saez and Thomas Piketty, "Income Inequality Update," *Daily Kos*, February 13, 2013, http://www.dailykos.com/story/2013/02/13/1186890/-Saez-Piketty-Income-Inequality-Update-Top-1-Have-Received-121-of-Income-Gains-Since-2009#.

8) Scharmer and Kaufer, *Leading from the Emerging Future*, 5.

9) "Matt Taibbi and Bank Whistleblower on How JPMorgan Chase Helped Wreck the Economy, Avoid Prosecution," *Democracy Now*, November 7, 2014, http://www.democracynow.org/2014/11/7/matt_taibbi_and_bank_whistleblower_on.

10) "Matt Taibbi and Bank Whistleblower."

11) "Matt Taibbi and Bank Whistleblower."

12) Jeffrey M. Lobosky, *It's Enough to Make You Sick: The Failure of American Health Care and a Prescription for the Cure* (Lanham, MD: Rowman and Littlefield, 2012), 14.

13) Lobosky, *It's Enough*, 56–57.

14) Jonathan Cohn, "Drug Deal," *New Republic*, August 25, 2009, http://www.newrepublic.com/article/politics/drug-deal.

15) Ryan Grim, "Internal Memo Confirms Big Giveaways in White House Deal with Big Pharma," *Huffington Post*, August 13, 2009, http://www.huffingtonpost.com/2009/08/13/internal-memo-confirms-bi_n_258285.html.

16) Sunlight Foundation, "Visualizing the Health Care Lobbyist Complex" (Sunlight Foundation, July 22, 2009), http://sunlightfoundation.com/tools/2009/healthcare_lobbyist_complex/.

17) Otto Scharmer, *Theory U: Leading from the Emerging Future* (Cambridge, MA: Society for Organizational Learning, 2007), 329.

18) The National Commission on Excellence in Education, *A Nation at Risk: The Imperative for Educational Reform* (Washington, DC: US Department of Education, 1983), 7, quoted in Gary Lamb, *The Social Mission of Waldorf Education: Independent, Privately Funded, Accessible to All* (Fair Oaks, CA: AWSNA, 2004), 52.

19) US Department of Education, *The National Goals for Education* (Washington, DC: US Department of Education, July 1990), quoted in Lamb 55.

20) US House of Representatives, *Goals 2000: Educate America Act* (Washington, DC: House of Representatives Conference Report, March 21, 1994), 4–5, quoted in Lamb 65–66.

21) 1996 National Education Summit Policy Statement, http://www.edweek.org/ew/articles/1996/04/03/28sumpol.h15.html, quoted in Lamb 69.

22) *1999 National Education Summit* (Washington, DC: Achieve, 1999), 4, quoted in Lamb 73.

23) *2001 National Education Summit* (Washington DC: Achieve, 2001), 2, quoted in Lamb 77.

24) "Executive Summary of the 'No Child Left Behind Act of 2001'" (Washington, DC: Business Roundtable, 2001), 1, quoted in Lamb 78.

25) Lamb, *Social Mission*, 81.

26) Ian Vandewalker, "The Consequences of 'Citizen United,'" http://www.msnbc.com/msnbc/the-consequences-citizens-united.

27) Jason Linkins, "The Supreme Court's *Citizen United* Decision Is Terrifying," *Huffington Post*, January 21, 2010, http://www.huffingtonpost.com/2010/01/21/the-supreme-courts-citize_n_432127.html.

28) Chris Cillizza, "How Citizens United Changed Politics, in 7 Charts," *Washington Post*, January 21, 2014, http://www.washingtonpost.com/blogs/the-fix/wp/2014/01/21/how-citizens-united-changed-politics-in-6-charts/.

29) Cillizza, "How Citizens United Changed."

Chapter 2

1) Luigi Morelli, *Legends and Stories for a Compassionate America* (San Francisco: Berrett-Koehler, 2014), 18–20.

2) Susan B. Martinez, *The Psychic Life of Abraham Lincoln* (Franklin Lakes, NJ: Career Press, 2009), 82.

3) Martinez, *The Psychic Life*, 83.

4) Martinez, *The Psychic Life*, 135.

5) Martinez, *The Psychic Life*, 106.

6) Martinez, *The Psychic Life*, 125.

7) William J. Wolf, *Lincoln's Religion* (Philadelphia: Pilgrim Press, 1970), 125.

8) Wolf, *Lincoln's Religion*, 135.

9) Wolf, *Lincoln's Religion*, 136.

10) Luigi Morelli, *A Revolution of Hope: Spirituality, Cultural Renewal and Social Change* (Bloomington, IN: Trafford, 2009), chapter 6.

11) William Ellery Channing, *Dr. Channing's Notebook: Passages from the Unpublished Manuscripts of William Ellery Channing*, ed. Grace Ellery Channing (Boston: Houghton, Mifflin, 1887), 96.

12) Alexis de Tocqueville, *Democracy in America* (Chicago: University of Chicago Press, 2000).

13) Ralph Waldo Emerson, "The American Scholar," *The Complete Essays and Other Writings of Ralph Waldo Emerson* (New York: Modern Library, 1950).

14) Emerson, "Intellect," *The Complete Essays*.

15) Emerson, "Uses of Great Men," *The Complete Essays*.

16) Alcoholics Anonymous World Services, *Pass It On: The Story of Bill Wilson and How the A. A. Message Reached the World* (New York: Alcoholics Anonymous World Services, 1984), 60.

17) Alcoholics Anonymous, *Pass It On*, 60.

18) Alcoholics Anonymous, *Pass It On*, 121.

19) Alcoholics Anonymous, *Pass It On*, 374.

20) Alcoholics Anonymous World Services, *Twelve Steps and Twelve Traditions*.

21) Derek Gill, *Quest: The Life of Elisabeth Kübler-Ross* (Brisbane, Australia: Australasian Book Society, 1981), 326–27.

22) Gill, *Quest*, 327.

23) Elisabeth Kübler-Ross, *On Life after Death* (Berkeley, CA: Celestial Arts, 1991), 24.

24) Emerson, "Uses of Great Men," *The Complete Essays.*

25) Alcoholics Anonymous, *Pass It On,* 275.

26) http://www.nderf.org/number_nde_usa.htm (from Near Death Experience Research Foundation website), quoted in "Key Facts about Near Death Experiences," http://www.iands.org/about-ndes/key-nde-facts.html?start=6 (from the International Association for Near-Death Studies website).

27) Morelli, *A Revolution of Hope,* chapters 4 and 5.

28) Benjamin Barber, *Jihad vs. McWorld: How Globalism and Tribalism Are Reshaping the World* (New York: Random House, 1995).

29) Felipe Fernandez-Armesto: *The Americas: The History of a Hemisphere* (New York: Random House, 2005).

Chapter 3

1) Marshall B. Rosenberg, *Nonviolent Communication: A Language of Compassion* (Encinitas, CA: Puddle Dancer Press, 1999).

2) For more on the history of the Ecumenical Institute/Institute of Cultural Affairs, see Luigi Morelli, "A Revolution of Hope: Spirituality, Cultural Renewal and Social Change" blog: http://luigimorelli.wordpress.com/2011/02/15/a-story-of-organizational-change-from-ecumenical-institute-to-fifth-city/ and http://luigimorelli.wordpress.com/2011/03/07/a-story-of-organizational-change-2-from-fifth-city-to-ica/.

3) Brian Stanfield, *The Art of Focused Conversation: 100 Ways to Access Group Wisdom in the Workplace* (Gabriola Island, Canada: New Society Publishers, 2000).

4) Peggy Holman, Tom Devane, and Steven Cady, *The Change Handbook: The Definitive Resource on Today's Best Methods for Enlarging Whole Systems* (San Francisco: Berrett-Koehler, 2007).

5) Otto Scharmer, *Theory U.*

6) Peter Senge, Otto Scharmer, Joseph Jaworski, and Betty Sue Flowers, *Presence: Exploring Profound Change in People, Organizations and Society* (New York: Doubleday, 2004), 111, 113, 222, and 234.

7) For the ten principles to which businesses need to subscribe in order to join the Global Compact, see: https://www.unglobalcompact.org/AboutTheGC/TheTenPrinciples/index.html.

8) Adam Kahane, *Power and Love: A Theory and Practice of Social Change* (San Francisco: Berrett-Koehler, 2010), chapter 6.

9) Tom Atlee, *Empowering Public Wisdom: A Practical Vision of Citizen-Led Politics* (Berkeley, CA: Evolver Editions, 2012), xx.

10) Expanded from Atlee, *Empowering Public Wisdom*, chapter 6.

11) Expanded from Atlee, *Empowering Public Wisdom*,, 124–26.

12) Expanded from Atlee, *Empowering Public Wisdom*,, 96.

13) Expanded from Atlee, *Empowering Public Wisdom*,, 12.

14) Expanded from Atlee, *Empowering Public Wisdom*,, 179.

15) David Graeber, "Enacting the Impossible: On Consensus Decision-Making," *Occupied Wall Street Journal*, no. 3 (September 2011), http://occupywallst.com/archive/Oct-2011/.

16) Nathan Schneider, "Occupy Wall Street: FAQ," in *Occupied Wall Street Journal*, no. 1 (October–November 2011).

Chapter 4

1) Peter Senge, Bryan Smith, Nina Kruschwitz, Joe Laur, and Sara Schley, *The Necessary Revolution: Working Together to Create a Sustainable World* (New York: Doubleday, 2008), 16.

2) Senge et al., *The Necessary Revolution*, 16.

3) Senge et al., *The Necessary Revolution*, 27–28.

4) Quoted in Margaret J. Wheatley, *Leadership and the New Science: Discovering Order in a Chaotic World* (San Francisco: Berrett-Koehler, 1999), 33.

5) Scharmer, *Theory U*, 51.

6) Scharmer, *Theory U*, 301–02.

7) Wheatley, *Leadership and the New Science.*

8) Joseph Jaworski, *Synchronicity: The Inner Path of Leadership* (San Francisco: Berrett-Koehler, 2011).

9) Jaworski, *Synchronicity*, 116.

10) Senge et al., *The Necessary Revolution*, 235.

11) Scharmer, *Theory U*, 212–13.

12) Adam Kahane, *Power and Love: A Theory and Practice of Social Change* (San Francisco: Berrett-Koehler, 2010), 105–13.

13) Senge et al., *The Necessary Revolution*, 235.

14) Senge et al., *The Necessary Revolution*, 250–51 and 260–61.

15) Sustainable Food Laboratory website: http://sustainablefood.org/component/content/article/22-main/258-inclusive-business-projects.

16) Sustainable Food Laboratory website, http://www.sustainablefood.org/projects.

17) David Cooperrider, "Fairmount Minerals Secret to Success: Combine High Engagement with Sustainable Design and High Integrity Leadership," http://www.davidcooperrider.com/2014/02/19/fairmount-minerals-secret-to-success-combine-high-engagment-with-sustainable-design-and-high-integrity-leadership/.

18) Senge et al., *The Necessary Revolution*, 286–89.

19) Senge et al., *The Necessary Revolution*, 182.

20) Senge et al., *The Necessary Revolution*, 109.

21) Senge et al., *The Necessary Revolution*, chapter 7.

22) Senge et al., *The Necessary Revolution*, 94.

23) Senge et al., *The Necessary Revolution*, 74.

24) "America's Cities 'LEED' the Way: The Green Building Movement Is Being Readily Adopted into Municipal Facilities," on Buildings. com, May 17, 2005, http://www.buildings.com/article-details/ articleid/2475.aspx.

25) Senge et al., *The Necessary Revolution*, 220.

26) Senge et al., *The Necessary Revolution*, 75.

27) Greenlivingpedia, a free resource for sharing information on green living, http://www.greenlivingpedia.org/Living_building.

28) R. Brian Stanfield, *The Courage to Lead: Transform Self, Transform Society* (Toronto: Canadian Institute of Cultural Affairs, 2000), 245.

29) Stanfield, *The Courage to Lead*, 244.

30) See the documentaries *Fifth City: A Decisional City* (1983), *The World of Human Development* (1977), and *Courage to Care* (1984), collected in the DVD *The World of Human Development: Origins of the Institute of Cultural Affairs* (2007), produced by the Institute of Cultural Affairs International.

31) Stanfield, *The Courage to Lead*, 144.

32) Stanfield, *The Courage to Lead*, 247.

Chapter 5

1) Jon C. Jenkins and Maureen R. Jenkins, *The Social Process Triangles* (Toronto: Imaginal Training, 1997).

2) Jenkins and Jenkins, *Social Process Triangles*, 9.

3) Jenkins and Jenkins, *Social Process Triangles*, 8.

4) Stanfield, *The Courage to Lead*, 151.

5) Jenkins and Jenkins, *The Social Process Triangles*, 24.

6) Stanfield, *The Courage to Lead*, 249.

7) Christopher Schaefer, "Toxic Excess: Income Inequalities and the Fundamental Social Law," *New View* (Autumn 2012).

8) Scharmer and Kaufer, *Leading from the Emerging Future*, chapter 2.

Conclusion

1) "Obama & McConnell Pledge Cooperation: Will Fast-Tracking Secretive TPP Trade Deal Top Their Agenda?" Democracy Now interview with Senator Mitch McConnell and Lori Wallach, November 6, 2014, http://www.democracynow.org/2014/11/6/ obama_mcconnell_pledge_cooperation_will_fast.

Bibliography

Alcoholics Anonymous World Services. *Pass It On: The Story of Bill Wilson and How the A.A. Message Reached the World.* New York: Alcoholics Anonymous World Services, 1984.

———. *Twelve Steps and Twelve Traditions,* New York: Alcoholics Anonymous World Services, 1981.

Atlee, Tom. *Empowering Public Wisdom: A Practical Vision of Citizen-Led Politics.* Berkeley, CA: Evolver Editions, 2012.

Barber, Benjamin. *Jihad vs. McWorld: How Globalism and Tribalism Are Reshaping the World.* New York: Random House, 1995.

Channing, William Ellery. *Dr. Channing's Notebook: Passages from the Unpublished Manuscripts of William Ellery Channing.* Edited by Grace Ellery Channing. Boston: Houghton, Mifflin, 1887.

Emerson, Ralph Waldo. *The Complete Essays and Other Writings of Ralph Waldo Emerson.* New York: Modern Library, 1950.

Fernandez-Armesto, Felipe. *The Americas: The History of a Hemisphere.* New York: Random House, 2005.

Gill, Derek. *Quest: The Life of Elisabeth Kübler-Ross.* Brisbane, Australia: Australasian Book Society, 1981.

Greenleaf, Robert, K, *Servant Leadership, a Journey into the Nature of Legitimate Power and Greatness.* New York, Paulist Press, 1977

Hawken, Paul, Lovins, Amory and Lovins, L Hunter, *Natural Capitalism: Creating the Next Industrial Revolution*. Boston, New York, London, Little, Brown and Company, 1999.

Holman, Peggy, Tom Devane, and Steven Cady. *The Change Handbook: The Definitive Resource on Today's Best Methods for Enlarging Whole Systems*. San Francisco: Berrett-Koehler, 2007.

Jaworski, Joseph. *Synchronicity: The Inner Path of Leadership*. San Francisco: Berrett-Koehler, 2011.

Jenkins, Jon, and Maureen Jenkins. *The Social Process Triangles*. Toronto: Imaginal Training, 1997.

Kahane, Adam. *Power and Love: A Theory and Practice of Social Change*. San Francisco: Berrett-Koehler, 2010.

Kübler-Ross, Elisabeth. *On Life after Death*. Berkeley, CA: Celestial Arts, 1991.

Lamb, Gary. *The Social Mission of Waldorf Education: Independent, Privately Funded, Accessible to All*. Fair Oaks, CA: AWSNA, 2004.

Lobosky, Jeffrey M. *It's Enough to Make You Sick: The Failure of American Health Care and a Prescription for the Cure*. Lanham, MD: Rowman and Littlefield, 2012.

Martinez, Susan B. *The Psychic Life of Abraham Lincoln*. Franklin Lakes, NJ: Career Press, 2009.

McCaffrey, Paul, ed. *Global Climate Change*. The Reference Shelf, vol. 78, no. 1. New York: H. W. Wilson, 2006.

Morelli, Luigi. *Legends and Stories for a Compassionate America*. San Francisco: Berrett-Koehler, 2014.

————. *A Revolution of Hope: Spirituality, Cultural Renewal, and Social Change.* Bloomington, IN: Trafford, 2009.

Rosenberg, Marshall B. *Nonviolent Communication: A Language of Compassion.* Encinitas, CA: Puddle Dancer Press, 1999.

Schaefer, Christopher. "Toxic Excess: Income Inequalities and the Fundamental Social Law." *New View* (Autumn 2012).

Scharmer, Otto. *Theory U: Leading from the Emerging Future.* Cambridge, MA: Society for Organizational Learning, 2007.

Scharmer, Otto, and Katrin Kaufer. *Leading from the Emerging Future: From Ego-System to Eco-System Economies.* San Francisco: Berrett-Koehler, 2013.

Senge, Peter, Bryan Smith, Nina Kruschwitz, Joe Laur, and Sara Schley. *The Necessary Revolution: Working Together to Create a Sustainable World.* New York: Doubleday, 2008.

Senge, Peter, Otto Scharmer, Joseph Jaworski, and Betty Sue Flowers. *Presence: Exploring Profound Change in People, Organizations and Society.* New York: Doubleday, 2004.

Stanfield, Brian. *The Art of Focused Conversation: 100 Ways to Access Group Wisdom in the Workplace,* Gabriola Island, Canada: New Society Publishers, 2000.

————. *The Courage to Lead: Transform Self, Transform Society.* Toronto: Canadian Institute of Cultural Affairs, 2000.

de Tocqueville, Alexis. *Democracy in America.* Chicago: University of Chicago Press, 2000.

Wheatley, Margaret J. *Leadership and the New Science: Discovering Order in a Chaotic World.* San Francisco: Berrett-Koehler, 1999.

Wolf, William J. *Lincoln's Religion*. Philadelphia: Pilgrim Press, 1970.

Documentaries

See *Fifth City: A Decisional City* (1983), *The World of Human Development* (1977), and *Courage to Care* (1984) in *The World of Human Development: Origins of the Institute of Cultural Affairs* (2007), a DVD produced by Institute of Cultural Affairs International.

Index

f denotes figure

promoting change in, 85–86
progressive taxation, 103
prototyping, 58, 58*f*, 59, 60
public sector, engagement of, 88–90
public wisdom, 39, 61, 65

Q

Quakerism, 37, 70
quantum mechanics, 76

R

Rabobank, 81
Rainforest Alliance, 81
rationalism, 18, 21
reflective level (response), as one
    aspect of communication, 52
Religious Studies I, 50, 91
renewable energy/resources, 86
representative democracy, 12, 61
"Requickening Address," 42
Revivalism, 18
A Revolution of Hope (Morelli), 17
Ritchie, George, 34
Ritual of Condolence, 41, 42, 71
Rosenberg, Marshall, 47
Rough, Jim, 64

S

SAA (Sex Addicts Anonymous), 27
sacred activism, 72
Saunders, Cicely, 30
Scharmer, Otto, 55, 56, 57, 71, 79, 81,
    90, 102, 103
Schneider, Nathan, 71
scientific materialism, 32
Seattle, Battle of, 34, 35, 101
Second Great Awakening, 18
secrecy, 106, 107, 108
seeing, x, xi, 58*f*, 77
self-empathy (self-connection), as one
    aspect of communication, 47, 48, 49*f*

self-expression, as one aspect of
    communication, 47, 49*f*
self-reinforcing change, 86
seminar method, 91
Senge, Peter, 79, 90
sensing, 57, 58*f*
Servant Leadership (Greenleaf), 79
Sex Addicts Anonymous (SAA), 27
Shakers, 19
SIA (Survivors of Incest
    Anonymous), 27
Silkworth, W. D., 23
slavery, 45, 60
Smith, Adam, 39, 74
Smith, Robert, 24, 46
Snowden, Edward, 106–107
social change, 36, 40, 94, 112
social compacts, 102
social experience, redefining of, 32–38
social innovation, 40, 41
social justice, 111, 112
social process triangles, 97–98, 98*f*,
    100*f*, 101, 102
social reality, 34, 46, 50, 75
social security, 103
social technology, 40, 47, 50–60, 67,
    69, 71, 110, 111
social transformation, 41–43
social utopias, 74
socialism, 39, 74–75, 105
societal renewal, 38
Society for Organizational Learning,
    60, 81
solitary reflection, 91
Sparrow, G. Scott, 34
spiritual movements, 17, 19
spirituality, 16, 24, 29, 30, 109. *See
    also* experiential spirituality;
    practical spirituality
St. Christopher's Hospice (South
    London), 30

Open Book Editions
A Berrett-Koehler Partner

Open Book Editions is a joint venture between Berrett-Koehler Publishers and Author Solutions, the market leader in self-publishing. There are many more aspiring authors who share Berrett-Koehler's mission than we can sustainably publish. To serve these authors, Open Book Editions offers a comprehensive self-publishing opportunity.

A Shared Mission

Open Book Editions welcomes authors who share the Berrett-Koehler mission—Creating a World That Works for All. We believe that to truly create a better world, action is needed at all levels—individual, organizational, and societal. At the individual level, our publications help people align their lives with their values and with their aspirations for a better world. At the organizational level, we promote progressive leadership and management practices, socially responsible approaches to business, and humane and effective organizations. At the societal level, we publish content that advances social and economic justice, shared prosperity, sustainability, and new solutions to national and global issues.

Open Book Editions represents a new way to further the BK mission and expand our community. We look forward to helping more authors challenge conventional thinking, introduce new ideas, and foster positive change.

For more information, see the Open Book Editions website:
http://www.iuniverse.com/Packages/OpenBookEditions.aspx

Join the BK Community! See exclusive author videos, join discussion groups, find out about upcoming events, read author blogs, and much more! http://bkcommunity.com/